D0850524

Politics and
Sexual Equality

Politics and Sexual Equality

The Comparative Position of Women in Western Democracies

Pippa Norris

Senior Lecturer in Government
Newcastle Polytechnic

Wheatsheaf
Books

RIENNER   Boulder, Colorado

First published in Great Britain in 1987 by
WHEATSHEAF BOOKS LTD
A MEMBER OF THE HARVESTER PRESS PUBLISHING GROUP
Publisher: John Spiers
16 Ship Street, Brighton, Sussex
and in the United States of America by
LYNNE RIENNER PUBLISHERS, INC.
948 North Street, Boulder, Colorado 80302

British Library Cataloguing in Publication Data
Norris, Pippa
   Politics and sexual equality: the
   comparative position of women in Western
   democracies.
   1. Women—Social conditions 2. Democracy
   I. Title
   305.4'2'091713   HQ1154

   ISBN 0–7450–0193–9

Library of Congress Cataloging in Publication Data
Norris, Pippa.
   Politics and sexual equality.

   Bibliography: p.
   Includes index.
   1. Women's rights 2. Women and politics.
3. Feminism. · I. Title.
HQ1236.N67   1987   323.3'4   87–9465
ISBN 1–55587–072–4   (Lib. BDG.)

Phototypeset in Linotron Times, 11 on 12 pt
by Input Typesetting Ltd, London
Printed in Great Britain by
Billing & Sons Ltd, Worcester.

Contents

Tables

Figures

1 Introduction: Comparative Sexual Equality

Twenty years after the start of the second wave of the women's movement we need to take stock of how far the lives of women and men have changed in Western countries. These decades have seen a range of significant developments in sexual equality since the publication of such seminal works as Betty Friedan's *The Feminine Mystique* in America, Simone de Beauvoir's *The Second Sex* in France and Germaine Greer's *The Female Eunuch* in Britain. Since the early 1960s widespread socio-economic trends, including dramatic increases in the number of working mothers, single-parent families and divorce rates in Western countries, have substantially affected the relationship between the sexes at work and in the home. These years have seen the growth of the second wave of the women's movement with groups developing in all countries from the National Organization of Women (NOW) in the United States and the National Women's Co-ordinating Committee (NWCC) in Britain to Dolle Mina in the Netherlands and the Women's Electoral Lobby in Australia. At the grassroots level there has been a proliferation of diverse organisations developed to offer practical support for women who need help with such problems as job discrimination, housing difficulties, rape or violence, as well as women's bookshops, art groups, cafes, publishing houses and child-care services. In addition to the emergence of self-help groups, these decades have seen significant developments in how far the state has responded to the problems of women with public policies on such issues as equal pay, sex discrimination and abortion. International organisations like the EEC and the

1

UN have also reacted to the pressure for social change, with initiatives such as the official Decade of Women (1975–85) declared by the United Nations.

What has been the net result of all these trends? We need to pause to take stock of developments, to see change in perspective, to draw up a rough balance-sheet of the gains and losses experienced by the women's movement over the last twenty years. This book aims to contribute to this overall assessment by comparing a range of twenty-four Western societies in recent decades to see where sexual stratification has altered most radically and, in particular, how far socialist parties have had a significant impact on the situation of women. Since the 1960s the situation of women has changed substantially, but whether this represents progress remains an open question: there are both optimistic and pessimistic assessments.

On the positive side of the balance-sheet many feel that in Western countries the relationship between the sexes has been transformed over the last decades, with a wider range of options open to women in their personal relationships, family lives, educational opportunities and occupational choices. Some of the most significant evidence in support of the positive assessment lies in the world-wide expansion of *de jure* women's rights over the last decades. By the mid-1980s 90 per cent of all countries had established official government bodies concerned with the advancement of women (United Nations 1985). The majority of countries have instituted constitutional and legal equality between women and men, whilst more than 67 countries have ratified or acceded to the UN Convention on the Elimination of All Forms of Discrimination Against Women (1979), becoming legally bound by its provisions to achieve equal rights for women in all fields—political, economic, social, cultural and civil. The review of the United Nations Decade for Women (1975–85) concluded that substantial progress had been made throughout the world in securing *de jure* equality for women, in terms of nationality, legal capacity, property ownership, freedom of movement and choice of name, with the Decade acting as a catalyst for legal reforms (United Nations 1985).

Others remain fairly sceptical, however, about how far

these initiatives have had a substantial impact on the lives of the majority of women. The range of statutes, collective agreements and constitutional conventions introduced to improve women's rights over the last decades may prove only symbolic without government commitment to the costs of implementation. Those who are more pessimistic about the direction and extent of change argue that despite the efforts of the women's movement the traditional patriarchal power structure remains both in the home and in the public arena so that there is a massive gap between *de jure* and *de facto* women's rights.

It is these changes which lie at the heart of this book which focuses on a range of twenty-four Western societies to examine two central questions. First, amongst capitalist democracies over the last decades, *where has there been most significant change in the position of the sexes*? Comparisons are complex, each society has its own cultural attitudes towards the role of the sexes. In each country the women's movement has a distinctive range of goals and aspirations. Governments have responded to the pressure for social change with a variety of policies and programmes. Yet there are enough similarities in such countries as Australia, the United States and Finland for us to attempt some comparisons concerning the position of women. We can start asking a number of questions. Where are reproductive rights still restricted? Where have substantial numbers of women reached the executive board-room? Where have they achieved parity on the shop floor? Where are women getting elected onto local councils? Where are women getting state-funded child-care? Where do men have paternity rights? Where have attitudes towards sex roles changed most radically? To make cross-cultural comparisons of sexual equality this study uses a range of economic, social, political and cultural indicators. The use of social indicators grew rapidly in the 1970s, but so far there have been few attempts to apply these methods systematically in order to compare the status of women. No single measure can reflect the complex position of the sexes in different societies, but multiple indicators using data accrued since the 1950s can provide the basis for a cross-national model of change over time.

On the foundation of these comparisons we can analyse whether there are any systematic patterns which explain *why* some societies have changed further and faster than others. In particular we can explore the second central question of this book: *how far have political parties had an impact on sexual equality*? We will examine to what extent, and in what circumstances, the political composition of governments is an important variable which accounts for observable differences in policy outputs and policy outcomes concerning sexual equality in capitalist democracies.

In theory we might expect that, given their egalitarian commitment, Socialist and Social Democratic governments would be more active in reducing sexual inequalities than more right-wing regimes. In capitalist democracies over the last decades there have been a wide range of policy initiatives to tackle the problems facing women, including policies on reproductive choice, sex discrimination in education, equal pay in the labour market, equal opportunities in training and promotions, violence in the home, and social services for child-care. Although changes have been implemented by all administrations, a large share of the credit has been claimed by Socialist governments. It was Mitterrand who initiated the Ministry for Women's Rights in France, Papandreaou, leader of PASOK, who created the Greek Council for Equal Rights, and the Labour Party which set up the Equal Opportunities Commission to monitor equal pay in Britain. Feminists who work within left-wing parliamentary parties, in a broad coalition with other disadvantaged groups, claim that this strategy can be an effective way to improve the position of women. Yet many other feminists are sceptical about how far political parties, as part of the patriarchal power structure, can have any fundamental impact on the position of women. Those who believe in the overthrow of capitalist patriarchy, or radical separatism or the conservative status quo, argue that Socialist governments can have little positive impact on social change through state interventionist policies. Within political science doubt has also been cast on the policy impact of political parties by a range of studies. In short, does comparative evidence suggest that parties matter for women? This question has significant theoretical and practical implications for feminists.

POLICY IMPACT MODEL

Any general discussion of the role of the state in changing sexual stratification has to be rooted in feminist theory, which will be discussed in detail in the following chapter. As we shall see, many feminists feel that a patriarchal state can only be expected to reinforce, rather than change, sexual inequalities. The immediate context of this study, however, is the extensive literature which has developed in political science concerning the effect of party governments on social equality, using local, national and cross-cultural comparisons. Considerable empirical research has developed to analyse policy outputs, although no consensus has emerged about the results of this work. In particular, academic controversy has centred around the rival claims of political and socio-economic variables in explaining social inequalities (for a review, see Kavanagh 1983; King 1981). In the context of this debate in political science we need to extend the methodology developed in the literature to see whether parties have an impact on *sexual* as well as social stratification. As a heuristic device, to simplify the complexities of the policy process, most studies have used a systems model to measure the association between selected environmental and political variables on policy outcomes, as illustrated in the flow chart in Figure 1.1.

ENVIRONMENTAL RESOURCES

Debate revolves around the question of whether environmental or political variables have most influence on the policy output in democracies. On the one hand, many writers emphasise the role of environmental resources such as the level of industrialisation, economic growth or affluence, on policy output. In the United States early

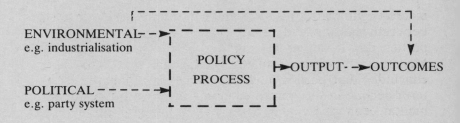

Figure 1.1 : Model of the policy process

studies by Dawson and Robinson (1963), broadly confirmed
later by Dye (1966), Sharkansky (1968), Hofferbert (1966)
and others (see King 1981), suggest that socio-economic
factors (per capita income, urbanisation and industrialisation) had more affect on state welfare expenditure than
political variables (party control, turnout, inter-party
competition). The central thrust of these studies is that the
policies adopted by American states can be predicted far
better by a knowledge of the state's economic and social
structure than by a knowledge of its politics. As Dye
concluded: 'On the whole economic resources were more
influential in shaping state policies than any of the political
variables previously thought to be important in policy determination.' (Dye 1976: 29).

It can be argued that the nature of the party system in
the United States means that this is a poor test of the effects
of left-wing mobilisation; however, studies in many other
countries tend to support the general conclusions. In
Britain, Richard Rose compared the policy outcome of
alternating Labour and Conservative governments over a
twenty-year period (Rose 1984). He found that economic
policy outcomes were largely unaffected by changes in party
government; instead, secular trends influenced the size of
the public-sector deficit, spending on social services, the
level of unemployment, economic growth and the redistribution of wealth. Rose argues that although British parties
claim to have different goals which they will implement,
when in office both Socialists and Conservatives are
constrained by circumstances from having a major impact on

macro-economic trends. We need, therefore, to distinguish between rhetoric and reality, what parties say and what parties do. Rose, in his analysis of the governments of Macmillan, Wilson, Heath, Callaghan and Thatcher, concludes that parties have been unable to halt the long-term decline in the British economy or to introduce fundamental economic changes, no matter their intentions and promises:

Much of a party's record in office will be stamped upon it by forces outside its control. British parties are not the primary forces shaping the destiny of British society; it is shaped by something stronger than parties. . . . The momentum of the economy continues to determine inputs and outcomes, whether the Chancellor of the Exchequer seeks guidance from a red or a blue book. (Rose 1984: 140–2)

These overall conclusions of the impact of political parties are supported in many wider comparative studies of industrialised societies. Cutright (1965), Parkin (1971), Wilensky (1975), Jackman (1980) and others (see King 1981) have tried to determine the correlates of social policy and income inequalities in a large number of countries. They found that the best predictors of levels of social-welfare expenditure were not political but environmental, including levels of socio-economic development, the structure of the population and the age of the social services programme. As Wilensky concluded:

Economic growth and its demographic and bureaucratic outcomes are the root cause of the general emergence of the welfare state. As for the political system and ideological factors, these categories are almost useless in explaining the origins and general development of the welfare state. (Wilensky 1975: xiii)

In other words, there were general pressures in all industrial societies for a common set of income-maintenance programmes which were independent of whether the political system was capitalist or communist, liberal democratic or authoritarian. Countries which are industrialised, affluent and urbanised have welfare-state and mixed-economy policies irrespective of party political factors. In the long run, political factors mattered, if at all, only in influencing the timing of the introduction of new social-welfare programmes.

Researchers have come to these conclusions from diverse intellectual backgrounds, derived from the theories of functionalism, the 'end of ideology' debate and neo-Marxism (Brooks 1983). The *functionalist* view argues that the needs of modern technology inherently lead to a certain type of social structure, irrespective of governmental aims to change society (Davis 1949; Parsons 1970). In this perspective the present system of social inequalities functions to produce differential rewards to recruit individuals to positions in an efficient manner. Political attempts to alter this social structure can have no lasting impact given the logic of modern industrialism (Kerr 1960). According to a number of observers the needs of modern technology and an advanced economy lead to a convergence of societies and gradually shape public policies in a similar pattern irrespective of political factors. For example, it can be argued that the expansion of the service sector and new technology led to a greater demand for women workers, hence equal-pay legislation was implemented to attract more women into the labour market. On this basis it can be suggested that economic developments were more influential in equal-pay policy than political factors, such as the strength of the women's movement or the role of left-wing parties.

The second view takes up Bell's thesis that there has been an *end of ideologically based politics* in pluralistic systems since the Second World War (Bell 1960; Christenson *et al.* 1971). Given the development of 'catch-all' parties, who try to win votes across all social groups, the partisan composition of governments will have little impact on social inequalities. For example, if policies such as equal-pay legislation attract widespread public support, and therefore votes, and the parties are largely indistinguishable ideologically, then we would not expect Social Democratic parties to have a stronger impact on inequalities than Conservative parties. Political pluralism serves to make significant redistributive efforts extremely difficult; any moves designed to benefit one disadvantaged group will be confronted by multiple groups offering strong opposition to threats to their established position.

Lastly, there is the *neo-Marxist* school, which includes a variety of arguments concerning the relative autonomy of the state but which tends to emphasise that in contemporary capitalist societies the mode of production predetermines to a large extent the outcome of social conflict. Political parties are marginal to the process of social change, compared with the underlying economic forces of social inequality (Gough 1979). Governments may ameliorate or exacerbate trends such as the growth of mass unemployment or the decline of manufacturing industry, but essentially they are powerless to reverse economic trends.

All of these theorists, for a variety of different reasons, agree that party politics does not matter. If we accept that parties can have little affect on policy outcomes, this would suggest that Social Democratic governments could have little impact on the position of women. They may claim to be more sympathetic towards women's issues, their rhetoric may be more egalitarian, but in practice they will be constrained from having a major impact on sexual inequalities. Instead, environmental variables will shape the position of women in each country. Socio-economic forces, including the demand for women in the labour market, the level of industrialisation, demographic trends, cultural expectations and economic growth, will be the primary variables determining such factors as the number of women in the workforce, their occupational pay and status, as well as child-support services, welfare benefits and reproductive rights. Given this perspective, if Social Democratic governments were strongly committed to reducing sexual inequalities, they would be powerless to do so, nor can we look primarily to the party system for social change. Instead, as many feminists argue, women have to work outside the formal governmental arena to achieve their objectives.

POLITICAL VARIABLES

This conclusion, however, remains controversial. Many disagree with the emphasis on environmental variables, suggesting that political explanations of policy outputs are more appropriate, including the influence of political parties, interest groups and the élite leadership. Political factors which have been emphasised include the degree of political institutionalisation; the extent of political centralisation (Wilensky 1975); the capacity of voters to influence party programmes through representative elections (Erikson 1978); the differential ability of political élites to respond to opportunities for 'political learning' (Heclo 1974); and the varied potential of interest groups to articulate and aggregate interests (Almond and Coleman 1960). For those who stress the influence of political factors on policy output, the role of political parties is seen as central. As a result, extensive research has concentrated on the policy effects of left-wing and right-wing parties at the local, state and national levels of government. Much recent research suggests that it can matter a good deal which party is in power in democracies.

Studies of the expenditure patterns by local authorities in Britain have found that there are variations in local services according to party control. Labour authorities spend more on council housing than Conservative authorities (Alt 1978; Boaden 1971) as well as more on education (Sharpe 1981; Sharpe and Newton 1984). In the United States political factors have also been found to be influential in state expenditure on welfare and educational policies (Sharkansky and Hofferbert 1968), as well as redistributive policies of taxes and benefits (Fry and Winters 1970).

This view is supported in cross-national comparisons where Hibbs (1977), Hewitt (1977), Schmidt (1985), Castles and McKinley (1979) and Dryzek (1978) have found that political variables were significant in explaining policy outputs and impacts. Hibbs found that in the 1960s in twelve Western nations Socialist governments tended to pursue policies leading to high inflation and low unemployment, contrary to centre and Conservative governments (Hibbs 1977). This study concludes that the macro-economic policies pursued by governments are largely in accordance with the interests of their class-defined core political supporters. In addition, Hewitt found a consistently positive association between left-wing party dominance in twenty-five Western states and egalitarian policies, reflected in the redistribution of incomes and access to higher education (Hewitt 1977). Cameron found that a sharper growth of the public sector from 1960 to 1975 was related to greater left-wing strength in government in eighteen Western societies (Cameron 1978). According to this array of studies, the control of government by different parties has a clear affect on policy outcomes.

If we accept these conclusions we might expect that Social Democratic governments could have an impact on public policies affecting sexual equality, if they were committed to transforming the lives of women and other disadvantaged groups. Some studies suggest this more specifically. Field, in a comparison of the abortion policies of twenty-nine nations found that in democratic societies, liberal policies on abortion were more frequently adopted by Socialists than by other parties, although the Catholicism of a country was the single most significant factor (Field 1979). She concluded: 'political institutions and ideologies do affect the nature and timing of policy decisions on abortion, contributing distinctively to policy differences across nations, at least in the short-run' (p. 779).

Lastly, Brooks, in his comparison of the impact of left-wing mobilisation in nineteen capitalist democracies, included a measure of sexual equality, defined as the ratio of males to females in terms of income and white-collar occupations (Brooks 1983). Given the breadth of the last category of work this operational criteria can be questioned; however, using it he found that between 1950 and 1970 sexual equality increased in fourteen of the nineteen nations compared with the largest gains in Japan, Sweden and Norway, and an actual decline in Canada, the USA, Ireland, France and Switzerland. On this basis the study concluded that there was a modest relationship between left-wing mobilisation and sexual equality.

These initial results are suggestive, but the research needs to be extended more widely to see whether Social Democratic governments are associated with change in the position of women in a wide range of economic, social and political dimensions. We need to see whether party control has any influence on the policy *output* (including spending on child-care services or legislation on sex discrimination, equal pay and abortion) and, more significantly on the policy *outcomes* (such as the ratio of male to female pay or the provision of child-care places). There can be a considerable difference between the two: governments may support rights for women in public resolutions, statutes and constitutional conventions, but unless they are prepared to follow through with implementation, these may prove empty gestures. Government may, for instance, legalise abortion, but at the same time restrict its availability by bureaucratic qualifying procedures, inadequate funding or the lack of appropriate medical services. More frequently they may pass comprehensive legislation against sex discrimination but fail to promote women where they have direct opportunities to do so—within their own ranks. It is not sufficient, therefore, to compare legislation in isolation from the policy outcome. Only by analysing *de jure* and *de facto* equality can we attempt to separate rhetoric from reality, to see whether Socialist parties have a significant impact on sexual equality. First we need to consider the debate within the wider context of Feminist theory to see why social-democratic feminists feel that political parties can play a vital role through the state in furthering sexual equality, whilst liberals, radicals and conservative critics are more sceptical about these claims.

2 Feminist Theories of Social Change

The question of socialism and the role of the state has always been controversial in feminist circles. Feminists agree that there are deep-rooted social, economic and political inequalities between the sexes which need to be changed, but they fundamentally disagree in their analysis of why this situation has come about and how far it could, and should, be altered through government policy. There is greater consensus about goals than tactics. The relationship between organised socialism and feminism has always been an uneasy one; in Simone de Beauvoir's words, the Left have proved themselves both the chosen friends and the worst enemies of the women's movement (de Beauvoir 1984). Whilst many feminists feel that women need to work within Social Democratic parties to achieve sexual equality through changes in public policy, others are sceptical about the effectiveness of this strategy. Some feminists feel that left-wing parties are as patriarchal as any others, run predominately by men and for men. In this view, Socialist parties may pay lip-service to the need to take account of women 'and other minorities', but their primary concerns are with the politics of class. In an intense debate within feminism many radicals argue that we cannot look to Social Democratic parties to change the system, as they are themselves part of the system. Many feminists feel that women need to work in autonomous self-help groups to improve their position rather than fruitlessly dissipating their energies within Socialist parties in an attempt to influence the traditional political system. Doubts about the impact of left-wing parties on sexual stratification are shared by certain Marxist, classical liberal and conservative theorists, for different reasons. Each of these provides an alternative perspective on the role of political parties in social change.

Within feminism five theoretical perspectives on the role of the state can be seen as analytically distinct: the social-democratic, Marxist, classical liberal, radical and conservative views. In practice these categories are not so clear-cut; there is considerable overlap between them, particularly on the question of practical policy goals. Most feminists cannot be neatly placed in one perspective, and there is considerable variation amongst advocates within each complex and evolving body of theory. (For a fuller account, see Spender 1985; Charvet 1982; Eisenstein 1984). This outline concentrates on the basic models which underlie the richer and more differentiated views of a wide range of authors. The constructed core theories cannot fairly represent the complexity and subtlety of feminist thought. It is important, however, to concentrate attention on a deliberately simplified set of feminist approaches to the role of political parties if we are to have any success in applying the theoretical models to empirical comparisons. In addition, philosophically each perspective has its roots in a different tradition of thought and can therefore be distinguished analytically by briefly contrasting selected seminal feminist writers on the role of the state.

COLLECTIVE NEEDS

Why do social democrats argue that left-wing parties can have a substantial impact on sexual stratification through positive government action? Essentially, socialists believe that the problem of equality is one facing women as a class which calls for collective solutions, with direct intervention by the state to change the conditions of sexual segregation. Socialism embraces a wide range of diverse groups, from revolutionary Trotskyists and communists to reformist Fabians and social democrats. There is considerable disagreement between them, but socialist feminists share the belief that equality of opportunity, which is the primary demand of classical liberal feminists, whilst useful, is only the first stage of change. Socialists argue that formal equal rights might gain access to the boardroom or the medical school for a few upwardly aspiring women but this is not enough in itself. Middle-class professional women with a successful career might gain in material rewards and social status but they are left with the double burden of job plus home responsibilities. If they are affluent, with a supportive spouse or enough money to pay for a child-minder, they can get by. But this does not help the mass of women who work in low-paid jobs and still have the main home responsibilities. Traditional attitudes need to change, but this will not affect the structural factors which act as constraints on what individual women can do within the present system. In socialist theory the nature of the problem is one that is on a social scale and therefore needs social solutions through public policy. For socialists who believe in the parliamentary route, working within Social Democratic parties in a broad left-wing alliance can be one of the most effective ways to improve the position of women.

The socialist feminist tradition stretches in a complex and evolving tradition from classical works by Karl Marx, Frederick Engels, August Bebel and Alexandra Kollontai, to more recent theorists such as Sheila Rowbotham and Juliet Mitchell (see Charvet 1982; Elshtain 1981). Socialism is a broad body of diverse thought, with complex controversies between social democrats, Fabians, Trotskyists, Leninists, Stalinists, and Maoists (see Berki 1975). There is also considerable overlap between socialist and radical feminists on the Left and liberalism on the Right. Given this complexity, we can start to distinguish socialist feminism theoretically by briefly outlining the origins of Marxist thought, before considering the practical reforms advocated by social democrats.

Marx did not discuss the equality of the sexes in detail in the main body of his work; however, Engels applied Marx's theoretical framework to women in *The Origins of the Family, Private Property and the State* (1884). For Engels the problems of women cannot be seen in isolation from the overall economic and social system. He felt that legal inequalities between the sexes were not the cause but the effect of economic oppression. Engels developed an analysis based on historical materialism to explain why sexual inequalities come about and how they can be changed. His argument, based on questionable anthropological evidence, is that in earlier communal societies both women and men contributed to the means of production so that there was relative equality between the sexes. The development of the division of labour led to greater inequalities, with women increasingly confined to the home while men controlled the primary means of production. The institution of monogamous marriages developed to meet the need to pass on property within the legal family.

As a result of these trends in developed societies, Engels argued, women suffer a triple burden, oppressed by domesticity, legal inequalities and capitalism. Sexism, like racism, is seen as functional for the capitalist economic system. The low pay given to women results in higher profits for companies, and the unpaid housework which women do is essential for society. The present family structure also supports the status quo as husbands who are the sole breadwinners cannot afford to strike nor change jobs so easily in the labour market. In this theory it is not individual men nor male supremacist ideas nor biology which determines the position of women; it is capitalism's need for a reserve army of labour, to keep wages down and profits up and for monogamous marriage to transmit accumulated property.

In this analysis it follows that only by changing the economic system can the position of women be transformed. As Engels wrote:

To emancipate woman and make her the equal of man is and remains an impossibility so long as the woman is shut out from social productive labour and restricted to private domestic labour. The emancipation of women will only be possible when women can take part in production on a large, social scale, and domestic work no longer claims anything but an insignificant amount of her time. (Engels 1884)

Under socialism domestic tasks would be placed on a collective basis with communal state-funded services for common needs such as the care and education of children and the production of food. Women would then be free of household work and able to participate equally in paid work in the public sphere. Engels is not very specific about how these arrangements would work in practice, along with other aspects of the communist society. He envisaged that it would still be predominately women who worked in the state nurseries, launderies and communal kitchens, although they would gain economic independence from their husbands through their work in a social industry. Marriage would be changed with the transformation of the family, with greater sexual freedom for both sexes and more liberal divorce. In short, Engels argued that equality of the sexes could only come about in a social system which recognised the need for structural change. Under capitalism legal reforms would not alter the fact that women are exploited in the factory and the home. Equality of opportunity might aid some middle-class professional women but it would not start to revolutionise the position of women as a group. The socialist solution to the women question is to liberate women from the private functions of wife and mother and make her into a public worker in the socialised economy. Women would therefore change to become more like men, but as radical critics have pointed out, there seems no analysis by Engels that in their sexual relationships men would also be transformed.

Engels's work in this area was neglected by many twentieth-century socialists who gave little priority to 'the woman question' until these ideas were revived by a number of recent theorists including Sheila Rowbotham in *Women, Resistance and Revolution* (1972), *Women's Consciousness, Man's World* (1972) and *Beyond the Fragments* (1979) and Juliet Mitchell's *Woman's Estate* (1971) and *Psychoanalysis and Feminism* (1975). Socialist feminists argue, along with Engels, that liberals who aim at token legal and political reforms without striving to transform the nature of the family and the economic system will fail to alter women's oppression. Fighting for free entry into the labour market will not improve the position of women unless housework is socialised, otherwise women merely end up with two jobs. In other words, this theory stresses that the state has to intervene directly to remove the structural constraints in women's lives. The liberal focus on equality of opportunity is insufficient; it is limited to the right to participate without systematic disadvantage in a meritocratic competition for individual, unequal rewards. In contrast, socialists argue that the aim should be for substantive equality for women as a group based on the equality of human needs (Nelson and Olesen 1977; Caulfield 1981).

For socialists who believe in the parliamentary route, there are a number of immediate practical measures which should be implemented. Social-democratic feminists stress that the government should do more for low-paid workers, for single-parent families and for the elderly, to stem the increasing feminisation of poverty. Amongst other priorities, cuts in social services have to be restored as these affect women in two ways, both as the main providers (nurses, teachers, social-workers) and users of welfare. Further, the assumptions built into the system of taxes and benefits should be revised, to get rid of the notion of 'breadwinner' and 'dependents', although the effects of such moves should be carefully monitored as the consequences may be detrimental to women. In matters of health-care and reproductive rights, there should be free contraception and abortion on demand through the health service, as well as a transformation of the power structure within medicine towards more patient control. In the education system there should be free day-care and nursery schools to transform women's 'double burden'. In the economy women could not rely on legal equality of opportunity, so state intervention should go further with affirmative action programmes and equal-worth legislation, implemented by an active administration. To achieve these aims socialist feminists believe that women cannot work in isolation but must create alliances with others in trade unions, the labour movement, and groups which are concerned with nuclear disarmament, the environment, poverty and urban deprivation. Only by co-operating with men in the working class, the poor, the blacks, the unemployed and other disadvantaged groups will women create an effective socialist society. Only by a broad strategy will feminism seem relevant for women facing the immediate problems of poverty, unemployment, bad housing and racialism. The strategy is one of co-operation with men, not separation. In this analysis it is not men as such who are the problem but the capitalist system which needs reforming (for social democrats) or overthrowing (for revolutionary socialists).

INDIVIDUAL RIGHTS

In contrast, both liberal and radical feminists doubt the efficacy of state action as a means of changing gender roles at a personal level. In its stead, liberals argue that the primary change has to come in the attitudes to gender roles acquired through our early socialisation, the family, education and the media. The classical liberal perspective is the one that is most pervasive in the West in a tradition which stretches in an unbroken line from John Stuart Mill's *The Subjection of Women* (1869) to Betty Friedan's *The Feminine Mystique* (1963) a century later. Indeed, Friedan reads at times like the ghost of John Stuart Mill, with a little more sex and sociology thrown in. Both focus on the problems of self-fulfilment which individuals experience when they fail to realise their full potential.

For Mill, women are brought up to restrict their real nature. Instead of developing the full range of their emotional and intellectual capacities, women are forced into a denial of themselves. Taught to believe that they can only live through their children and husbands, they become dependent and submissive. They learn to be obedient slaves, with social controls reinforced by the legal institution of marriage which, at the time, denied women any rights over their property and their children, and even failed to provide protection from brutal violence. Mill argued passionately that the situation should change to let women develop their full potential both for the benefit of women and that of society as a whole. The solution for Mill was for the state to remove the legal restrictions which denied women equal civil and political rights. They should have the same opportunities as men to vote and to participate in public life, to have access to property, to education and to professional occupations. Given these opportunities, especially in education, Mill felt that the position of women would change over time. These ideas were radical for Victorian

England but Mill did not go on to propose any fundamental change within the family. He felt that giving women equal rights to work, to divorce and to property would make marriage more of a matter of choice. If, however, women chose family life, then he saw a continuation of the traditional division of labour. Certainly, the state should not go beyond its proper boundaries to do more. In short, Mill argued that the law should recognise that there are no inherent differences between the sexes. Individuals should have equal rights, but the government should not intervene further in creating social equality. The rest was a matter of individual choice.

While Betty Friedan was speaking to a very different audience, her basic argument in *The Feminine Mystique* follows a very similar analysis. For Friedan, 'the problem which has no name', which she uncovered in middle-class suburbia in the 1960s was simply the fact that American women were kept from growing to their full human capacities (Friedan 1963: 318). Restricted by the world of home and children, the women she met found no inner fulfilment in their lives, they suffered a lack of identity, creativity and purpose. Echoing Mill, she found that women at home have become 'dependent, passive, childlike, they have given up their adult frame of reference to live at the lower human level of food and things . . . a slow death of mind and spirit' (p. 266). Lacking any intellectual challenge, women fail to develop their full range of abilities, and instead of the 'happy housewife' reflected in media images, they found a life of emptiness and dissatisfaction. Even that which was left, the emotional and sexual side of life, failed to provide fulfilment when given such unbalanced emphasis. The solution for Friedan, as for Mill, was self-development and personal growth through the challenge of education and work.

The role of the state was to ensure that women had equal rights to opportunities in colleges and the professions so that women could develop their latent abilities. In the liberal tradition, the state should remove barriers to individual achievement through creating legal equality, preventing employment discrimination and, to a limited extent, supporting the conditions for female work, such as facilitating child-care. Women should be able to compete with men on an equal basis if they wanted careers and conventional success. While the role of the state is primarily restricted to guaranteeing individual rights, women can only make full use of opportunities within the system. Other social change had to be a matter of altering prevailing attitudes so that women and men would realise how they could both benefit from less rigid sex roles. Once it was understood that women could make a valuable contribution to companies and professions, then discrimination would diminish. Once men came to see that they could develop their more expressive side through taking a greater role in childrearing, they would opt for greater partnership in marriage. Once children were raised with different expectations about their sex roles, they would take for granted more egalitarian relationships. The enemy was prejudice; the solution was enlightenment with the backing of legal equality of opportunities.

RADICAL SEPARATISM

But will a change in the legal or economic system bring about an end to the domestic exploitation of women? Will it be sufficient to transform our social relationships? For radical feminists the kind of equality suggested by equal-rights feminists is undesirable and male-defined. Its aim is for women to be equal to compete with men on their own terms, rather than the fundamental transformation of masculinity and femininity. Radicals feel that women should not model themselves on male behaviour, which is often undesirable; instead, they should develop a woman-centred analysis which values female qualities such as nurturance, co-operation and non-aggression. Female differences should not be eliminated in an androgenous model of equality but celebrated as a source of strength. For radical feminists the problem which women face is not the result of legal inequalities or the capitalist system, the problem is reproduction and the family.

Radical feminism is a complex and evolving body of

thought; there is considerable overlap with socialist feminism, but theoretical distinctions can be drawn. Radicals like Shulamith Firestone in *The Dialectic of Sex* (1971) and Kate Millet in *Sexual Politics* (1971), along with later writers such as Adrienne Rich, Nancy Chodorow and Mary Daly take as a central tenet that the present system of power is patriarchal, controlled by men for their own interest, and this is true of both capitalist and socialist countries (Eisenstein 1984). We cannot look to Social Democratic parties to change the system, for, as I have said they are themselves considered to be part of the problem. In Firestone's view, class inequalities need to be abolished, racial inequalities need to be eradicated, but behind both of these are more fundamental sexual inequalities. For radicals, male dominance is the oldest and most fundamental form of inequality. Unless revolutionaries abolish social institutions like the family and the school, they may change capitalism but sexism will remain. For Robin Morgan, a Marxist revolution would only be another coup d'état among men (Morgan 1977). The critique of socialist feminism is that it is insufficiently radical, it fails to recognise that sexual oppression is the fundamental source of all other oppressions, including class. For Morgan, 'Sexism is the root oppression, the one which, until and unless we uproot it, will continue to put forth the branches of racism, class hatred, ageism, competition, ecological disaster, and economic exploitation' (Morgan 1977). If sexism is such a pervasive and universal phenomenon, how do we account for its origins? In Firestone's analysis the original cause of woman's oppression was her childbearing and childrearing roles, it was woman's reproductive biology which introduced inequalities between the sexes: 'Nature produced the fundamental inequality—half of the human race must bear or rear children for all of them—which was later consolidated, institutionalised, in the interests of men' (Firestone 1971: 232). If the problem has biological roots, to change the situation women need to control the means of reproduction, which includes the use of technological developments to revolutionise the process of childbirth. Firestone criticised the socialist advocacy of day-care centres, arguing that this still puts the primary burden of child-care on women. We need to turn to medical and technological developments which will revolutionise the process of childbirth and abolish the family, 'the source of all psychological, economic and political oppression' (Firestone 1971). For Firestone, revolutions to date have been failures because the repression of women and children will go on so long as the family continues. Further, we cannot look to the bureaucratic state for radical change as it is itself an instrument of patriarchy; it functions to preserve the status quo of male power. The structure of benefits in the welfare state, for example, are frequently determined by marital status, which serves to strengthen and maintain the traditional family unit.

Other well-known radicals, such as Kate Millet in *Sexual Politics*, also emphasise that women's oppression is most firmly rooted within the family, and this has to be the starting point for any analysis of power inequalities. Public institutions are patriarchal, power lies in male hands in industry, technology, the military, universities, science, political parties and government. The chief institution of patriarchy, however, is the family, which 'is both a mirror of and a connection with the larger society; a patriarchal unit within a patriarchal whole. Mediating between the individual and the social structure, the family effects control and conformity where political and other authorities are insufficient' (Millet 1971: 33). As head of the family the father governs the members as the state governs society. Patriarchy ensures its continuing survival through the socialisation of the young into traditional roles. So how could patriarchy be abolished? Millet stresses that a revolution would require an end to traditional sexual inhibitions and taboos, particularly those which threaten monogamous marriage. Sexual freedom would undermine the traditional family and bring to an end the ideology of male supremacy and socialisation into segregated gender roles. The focal points for radical change are the institution of marriage, the family, sexuality and the control of reproduction.

In terms of strategy, radical feminists emphasise that feminists cannot expect male radicals, let alone Social Democratic parties, to co-operate with the women's movement, as it is directly against their interests. What is needed, at least in the first stage, is separatism; women have to work with women in self-help, non-hierarchical groups to achieve their own solutions in their own way. The women's movement should be autonomous, and women have to experience separatism in their own lives, with an emphasis on lesbianism. Participating in the system of patriarchy within governments or corporations will not transform the position of women as these institutions function to maintain the male power base. In the radical view, token women are allowed to enter centres of power, such as the media, parties, trade unions or parliaments, but this only serves to legitimate the system, as women have to play by the dominant male rules of the game. Feminists who wish to challenge patriarchy are not allowed into these institutions. Those like Mary Daly are particularly critical of women who are successful within the system, as doctors, lawyers or politicians, as she feels this is tokenism; a few women are allowed into pieces of patriarchal territory as a show of female presence (Daly 1978). Radicals further argue that feminists should not aim for an androgynous future in which women are similar to men, as there are many aspects of men's lives which are highly undesirable. Women should not work to be equally competitive, aggressive and exploitative. Instead, they should create a woman-centred analysis which values distinctive female qualities, including nurturance and co-operation. In this radicals part company with both liberals and socialists, for the emphasis is on the value of female differences rather than similarities with men. It is suggested that women have a distinctive set of moral values, pacific, co-operative, and creative, which Daly suggests should be developed in an entirely separate and self-contained women's culture.

In practical campaigns many radicals work with other feminists for change through the state, including loose alliances with Social Democratic and Socialist parties, primarily on matters of sexuality and reproduction, including abortion, pornography, rape and violence against women, but this is not their primary focus as they feel that overall legislation is a limited route to change. In support, radicals point to the apparent ineffectiveness of legislation as a means of achieving equal economic rewards. In the United States, for example, there as been an Equal Pay Act for over twenty years, but during this time there has been no major change in female wages; women are still taking home on average 60 cents for every male $1. Radicals agree with socialists that capitalism has to be transformed, but they argue that this will only take the women's movement so far. It is a necessary but not sufficient condition for achieving sexual equality. Revolutionary change can only come about through a radical transformation of the family and sexual relationships. Further, far from focusing on the state, gender change has to start in everyday lives; for radicals, 'the personal is the political'. Inequalities of power are experienced in public institutions but also directly in personal relationships. Unless women start to change their immediate lives, starting with their husbands, lovers and friends, how can they hope to change society? For radicals, it is just as important to understand the politics of housework as the conventional study of parties, pressure groups and parliaments. Feminists need to redefine 'politics' to perceive how male power operates at all levels. As a consequence of this analysis, radicals argue that feminist organisations should not reproduce the decision-making hierarchies found elsewhere; instead, women should work together in leaderless, decentralised groups which promote co-operation, equality and the development of a distinctive female culture.

THE CONSERVATIVE STATUS QUO

In response to the feminist debate, conservative theorists expressed strong doubts about how far traditional gender roles could, and should, be transformed. In many ways they share with the radicals the view that women have a distinctive role, one which should be highly valued in society. Amongst the most well known of these theorists are Steven Goldberg in *The Inevitability of Patriarchy* (1977) and Lionel Tiger in *Men in Groups* (1970). According to Goldberg, as a universal scientific law all known societies are patriarchal, whether the society is developing or industrialised, past or present, traditional or revolutionary. By patriarchal he means a system of hierarchical organisation (political, economic, industrial, financial, religious or social) in which the overwhelming number of upper positions are occupied by males. For Goldberg, authority and leadership are, and always have been, male dominated. Matriarchies are mythical, there is no sound anthropological evidence that they ever existed. Further, Goldberg believes that there are other universal gender differences. He argues that every society gives higher status to male roles than to the non-maternal roles of females. It does not matter what tasks are being done, whether cooking or surgery, outside of the family in every society the occupations filled by men are given high status. Goldberg believes that the areas where women are given the most prestige are those associated with their traditional roles in the care and rearing of the young. Nowhere are many women successful in competing with men in the public sphere:

In every society that has ever existed one finds patriarchy (males fill the overwhelming percentage of upper hierarchical positions in political and all other hierarchies), male attainment (males attain the high-status roles, whatever these may be in any given society), and male dominance (both males and females feel that dominance in male–female encounters and relationships resides in the male, and social expectations and authority systems reflect this). (Goldberg 1977: 63)

If these social patterns are universal, why is this? According to Goldberg the male has a stronger dominance tendency, which is the result of physiological differences between males and females. Biologically, males are more aggressive in attaining hierarchical positions. For the purposes of this discussion, the essential point of the theory is the assertion that sexual physiological differentiation leads inevitably and universally to differences between males and females. If this is the case, then nowhere are most women going to change traditional sex-roles to achieve equality with men in public power, status and rewards. As Goldberg concludes, we cannot change physiological differences between males and females which are the result of centuries of evolution. 'At the bottom of it all, man's job is to protect women, and woman's is to protect her infant; in nature all else is luxury' (p. 194). Our biological natures mean that men and women are different but complementary. In this theory woman's greatest strength is not to compete for male goals, where she will lose, but to cultivate her natural feminine role in the nurturance of the species. Attempts to make traditional sex roles more egalitarian will therefore fail, as patriarchy, male dominance and male status in suprafamilial roles are inevitable.

THEORETICAL PERSPECTIVES ON SOCIAL CHANGE

From these contrasting perspectives it is clear that theorists see the nature of the problem of sexual equality and its solutions in very different ways. Both liberals and socialists emphasise the similarities between the sexes, sharing an ideal of androgyny. Their aims are sexual equality, to give women and men equality of opportunity or of rewards. In contrast, both radical feminists and conservative critics suggest an ideal of sexual differences, that we should value that which is distinctive in women.

There is equally strong disagreement about how far changes in public policy introduced by Social Democratic governments could bring about feminist goals in capitalist democracies. Liberal feminists argue that policies which ensure equal rights and opportunities in education and employment would be effective by allowing women to compete equally in the job market, which in the longer term would transform stereotyped ideas about sex roles. On other major issues, like reproductive rights, the classical liberal view is that women are entitled to choose an abortion if they so wish but it is not necessary for the government to subsidise this service. In contrast, social democrats argue that the government needs to take an active, positive role in creating equality. Social democrats argue that there should be state-funded crèches and nursery schools as part of the educational system, and free abortion and contraception as part of the health service. To prevent the increasing feminisation of poverty the government should extend the welfare system with more generous help for single-parent mothers, widows and pensioners and those in low-paid jobs. As well as working through the conventional party system, women need to create alliances with the labour movement, trade unions, the anti-nuclear movement, environmentalists, anti-racist groups and others on the Left to improve the position of all oppressed groups. In contrast, radical feminists argue that the role of the state in creating social change is limited. The legal system can significantly restrict women, particularly in controlling matters like reproductive choice and sexual freedom, but as a part of the patriarchal power structure women cannot look to the government for positive change. Instead, women have to work with women to directly transform their situation, as Daly suggests, retreating from public campaigns to an inner metaphysical journey. Lastly, conservatives argue that, given our sexual-physiological natures, there can be no fundamental positive change in traditional sex roles. They believe that positions of public power and status are universally dominated by men in all societies. Conservatives feel that the state can legalise equality of opportunity, but the state is not God, it cannot alter our fundamental biological nature to make women and men the same, nor would this be desirable.

A central question raised by this theoretical debate is how far, in a range of capitalist democracies, Socialist governments have had a major impact on sexual stratification though public policy initiatives. Today the situation of women is strikingly different in societies as diverse as Sweden and Ireland or the United States and Japan. Why? Has this been the result of positive state action, or of wider social, cultural and economic trends? To examine this we need to turn to a consideration of how sexual equality can be compared on a systematic basis.

3 Social Indicators of Sexual Equality

If certain Western societies have experienced significant changes in sexual stratification in the last decades whilst others have been fairly static how can this be measured systematically? How do we compare the status of women in societies as diverse as Italy, the United States, Sweden and Ireland? We need to develop indicators which are multidimensional and reliable guides to sexual equality.

Studies of social stratification have generally focused on the three dimensions of social relations suggested by Max Weber: the distribution of rewards, prestige and power. Stratification exists where access to these goods is differentiated in a systematic way, on the basis of occupational class, racial origin, ownership of property, age, religious preference or sexual identity. Where there are systematic social inequalities between women and men in the distribution of rewards, prestige and power then, as Schlegel has suggested, this results in sexual stratification (Schlegel 1977). On this basis an *egalitarian society* will be understood to be *one where sex roles are highly similar in that which society values*.

The argument is not that it is necessarily desirable for women to have the *same* position as men in all areas of life; it can be questioned whether a society where women constitute half of the prison population, military casualties or heart-attack victims represents progress. Sexual equality is a complex concept; when feminists argue that women should be equal they rarely mean that women should aim to be identical to men, or treated in exactly the same way where there are relevant differences. The central focus of

this analysis concerns the empirical question of which countries are most egalitarian in the sexual distribution of that
which is most valued by society: whether financial rewards,
social   status,   educational   qualifications,   individual
autonomy, sexual freedom or political power. By itself no
single measure could reflect the multiplicity of women's
roles or the complexity of social change. We need multiple
indicators which can be applied cross-culturally to gauge
economic, social, political and cultural trends in sexual
equality over the last decades.

SOCIAL INDICATORS

The social-indicator movement originated in the 1960s in the
United States; it quickly led to the publication of systematic
social reports in Britain, West Germany and France, and the
involvement of organisations concerned with standardising
international statistics like the United Nations (United
Nations 1984a, 1984b). The aim of the movement was to
develop comprehensive and integrated quantitative measures using social and economic data to analyse such
phenomena as the quality of life, the general welfare of a
community or the social health of a nation. Indicators use
data which is relatively easy to observe to point to underlying processes which are harder to measure, such as sexual
equality or urban deprivation. They can be seen as signposts; their value depends on the closeness of fit between
the quantitative measure and the qualitative concept which
they represent (Deutsch 1980; Crawley 1981).

    Given existing social and economic data, the problem is
to select indicators of sexual equality which are valid and
reliable, which have broad applicability and wide appeal,
and which can be applied to policy outputs and policy
outcomes. Good social indicators should ideally meet the
criteria recommended by such bodies as the Organisation
for Economic Co-operation and Development (OECD
1981). To see the effects of policy, indicators should be
designed to describe social outputs rather than inputs, for
example the proportion of children in day care rather than

the amount of money being spent on such services. They should be non-institutional and applicable over long periods of time in different countries so that social trends can be analysed using comparable data. Indicators should describe prevailing social conditions which are potentially amenable to improvement in order to be relevant to public policy. Lastly, they should be comprehensive in coverage to describe social phenomena as an interrelated whole (OECD 1982). Good social indicators should allow change in the comparative position of women to be systematically monitored over the last decades to evaluate the impact of policies and programmes in creating equality.

The social-indicator approach has both advantages and disadvantages. Comparisons can be made on a more descriptive basis, looking in detail at the lives of women in major European countries (Steiner 1977) or using binary comparisons between Britain and the United States concerning the development of the women's movement (Bouchier 1983) or equal-pay policy (Meehan 1985; Ratner 1980). Other writers have focused on alternative areas: family and child-care policy in Sweden, the United States and China (Adams 1980; Ruggie 1983) or the comparative politics of abortion (Francome 1984; Lovenduski and Outshoorn 1986) or the position of women in power élites (Kohn 1980; Epstein and Coser 1981) or their political rights (Flanz 1983; Milburn 1976). There have also been a number of studies bringing together national writers discussing on a country-by-country basis the women's movement (Bradshaw 1982; Morgan 1984) women in politics (Lovenduski and Hills 1981), the role of women in development (Tinker *et al.* 1976; Benevia 1982) or the general position of women in each society (see, for example, Schlegel 1977; Patai 1967; Matthiasson 1974; Rohrlich-Leavitt 1975; Newland 1979; Iglitzin and Ross 1976; Giele and Smock 1977; Seward and Williamson 1970). This growing literature, particularly in the field of anthropology, provides fruitful insights into cross-cultural contrasts. Case studies and binary comparisons give a great wealth of detail about subtle differences which are washed out of the picture in a broader canvas. To make reliable generalisations about the impact of political factors on sexual equality, however, we need to supplement two or three country studies with wider longitudinal and cross-cultural comparisons (Dogan and Pelassy 1984).

Theoretically there are three primary goals guiding attempts to compare the status of women. First, to establish how far sexual inequalities are universal, with differences apparent in all the countries under comparison, for example in economic rewards or educational opportunities. Second, where there are variations the aim is to analyse how far they are systematically related to other variables, such as political or environmental factors. Lastly, to see how far idiosyncratic differences in sexual inequalities can be explained by particular social characteristics, such as public policy specific to one country. The study focuses on capitalist democracies over the last twenty years as this is the period during which the second wave of the women's movement has been most active and governments have introduced a range of policy initiatives on matters from equal pay to reproductive rights. As recognised by the 1985 United Nations Women's Conference in Nairobi, it is time to take stock of what has, and what has not, changed in recent years. A retrospective allows us to re-evaluate the past and provide markers for future trends.

It can be suggested that we are now moving towards the second stage of women's studies. In the first we were primarily concerned with documenting the position of women, given their invisibility in traditional disciplines such as history, political science and economics (Spender 1981; Langland and Gove 1981). Where we had little reliable information, we needed to describe the complex roles of women in each society, such as establishing the proportion of female representatives in local and regional government, or documenting the division of labour within the home, or the incidence of domestic violence. We needed a sceptical approach to previous research, critically re-examining the evidence for implicit assumptions (Eichler 1980). The first stage of women's studies research is far from complete; there are still many areas where we lack basic descriptive information. However, we can build on work done over the last decades to move towards the second stage of women's studies. This is concerned less with the description of the position of women in each society than with broader comparative explanations. There has developed a growing international network of women who are activists, public policy-makers and social scientists, brought into increasing contact by the activities of the United Nations Decade of Women, the organisations of the European Community and international conferences such as the World Congress on Women. International linkages have been strengthened in the women's movement, which has facilitated the interchange of research and information.

As a result of this collaborative work, we have started to establish some broad generalisations about the status of women. For example, it has not been confirmed in a number of studies that more women are elected under proportional representation than under majoritarian systems of elections. Why is this? Then again, equal-pay legislation has been introduced in all Western societies; where is it most successful and why? Abortion is now legalised in most but not all developed countries; why is this? It can be suggested that only a comparative perspective, building on a foundation of single-nation studies, can throw light on these sorts of significant questions. We know little about the nature of women and the extent to which the sexes are differentiated. All that we know, as John Stuart Mill pointed out in his classic study, is women and men as they appear in social environments (Mill 1974). The only way we can find out the nature of anything is to see how it reacts in different circumstances. Social scientists cannot usually control the environment, but they can observe variations in the environment and note their effects on the object under study. Comparisons allow us to observe differences between women and men under contrasting social circumstances, so that we can understand more clearly the nature of gender differences. The position of women varies in each society, but it is rarely unique, so we can start to analyse the similarities using techniques such as social indicators.

Social indicators can be seen as necessarily blunt but effective measures of the position of women relative to men in a wide variety of countries. They are one approach to comparative studies, to be supplemented by other methods for a more comprehensive analysis. They are limited by the *availability* and *accuracy* of data. In terms of availability there are many important aspects of sexual equality which are simply immeasurable or for which we have no reliable data covering all capitalist democracies, such as accurate information on the incidence of rape, incest, battery, sexual harassment or the division of household chores, although in response to the latter, comparative research into the use of time has developed (Szalai 1972). Some might feel that having to ignore the many unquantifiable aspects of sexual roles invalidates the approach. In reply it has to be said that, if used with sensitivity, indicators can provide signposts for change in many central aspects of women's lives, such as how much they earn, how many women are elected to power and how they feel about the women's movement. Indicators do not describe the detailed terrain but they give a contoured map which can be used for further exploration. There has also been progress towards comparability. International agencies such as the United Nations have recognised the need for social indicators on all aspects of women's lives, as a necessary basis for the formulation and evaluation of policies, and to this end it has created a new data-bank on the status of women (United Nations 1985d). Over the last decades more data has become available as individual governments have become aware of the need to provide sex-segregated official statistics and an invaluable contribution has been made by the network of women who collaborated on *Sisterhood is Global* (Morgan 1984). Researchers have started to develop social indicators of the status of women both comparatively (Boulding *et al.* 1976) and for specific countries (Ferriss 1971). Therefore, whilst much information on sexual stratification is still lacking, over the last decades considerably more statistical data has become available for analysis.

Accuracy is a problem since sex-based stereotypes and cultural preconceptions continue to affect the design of censuses and surveys (Oakley and Oakley 1979; United Nations 1984b; Morgan 1984). Conventional statistics can often be misleading; for instance, women's participation in the rural economy is frequently underreported because of their status as unpaid family workers on farms and smallholdings. There is no standard international definition of such categories as 'unpaid family workers', most of whom are women. Much female activity is ignored as a contribution to the economy, such as women's work as home-makers or in the care of elderly parents. Statistical concepts, such as the definition of 'head of household', can have an inherent sex bias. The concept of family head is based on the assumption that men head all nuclear families in the traditional breadwinning role while women take care of reproduction and home-care. The concept is based on a stereotyped view of the ideal family unit which does not take account of today's social realities, the large number of households made up of single persons living alone or with sole responsibility for children. This has been officially recognised by the census departments of Canada, Sweden, the United Kingdom and the United States who have pressed with some success for the replacement of the term in data collection in countries within the Economic Commission for Europe. The category of 'unemployed worker' is another problematic area, since this rarely includes discouraged job-seekers, the underemployed, such as part-time workers who would like to work full-time, or seasonal agricultural workers, many of whom are women. Official statistical sources are often far from ideal for these reasons, but if we are sensitive to their limitations there are a number of sources of data that can be utilised (United Nations 1984b).

Accuracy can be a problem if single indicators are selected to gauge complex concepts when other data needs to be taken into account; for example, measuring employment equality between the sexes by equal pay alone, which ignores hours of work, job conditions, future earnings and career prospects. The same problem of fractional measurement can be brought about by aggregating a number of distinct indicators into a single index since the relative trend of each component is hidden (Cazes 1972); for example, by making an overall index of sexual equality where the social, political and cultural indicators are given the same weight. Individual indicators of women's status, such as the labour-force participation rate of women, can be misleading by themselves. This indicator would suggest that there is something inherently preferable in labour-force work, no matter the pay or conditions. Only when this indicator is used in conjunction with others can we use it to assess the economic position of women. There is also the ethnomethodological problem of selecting indicators derived from one culture and applying them comparatively where they may be inappropriate. This problem is lessened by restricting comparisons by region or area, thereby avoiding extreme contrasts between developing and industrialised nations or those in the East and West. The focus on capitalist democracies gives us a relatively homogenous set of countries to compare, and it will be argued that the selected indicators of sexual equality, such as the ratio of male to female pay, are valid cross-culturally. Bearing in mind these limitations, with careful use multiple social indicators can provide a broad profile which supplements more qualitative approaches.

MEASURES OF SEXUAL EQUALITY

If we accept this argument, what measures should be selected as social indicators to gauge equality between women and men? Previous attempts to develop a status-of-women index have often been limited in their demographic data and their time-span. Ruth Dixon has suggested as an analytical framework that any yardstick of sexual equality would have to take account of gender differences in the spheres of reproduction, home-making, child-care, economic productivity, sexual relations and political decision-making (Dixon 1976). The basic premise of the model is that sexual equality only occurs with the abolition of the social division of labour based on gender. In other words, equality means a 50:50 distribution of men and women in all social areas so both sexes are equally represented in different roles and equally rewarded materially, socially and psychologically for their performance in these roles. The proposed model is suggestive but it needs to be developed with specific indicators for which quantitative data are available.

Others who have attempted an applied analysis have used a similar range of demographic measures; for example, Van Dusen and Sheldon used data on education, marriage, child-bearing and labour-force participation to examine changes in the lives of women in America (Van Dusen and Sheldon 1976), although they did not attempt a cross-cultural study. Youssef and Hartley applied demographic indicators of marital status, education, fertility and labour-force participation to eighty countries; however, the chosen measures were too blunt to make any clear distinctions between developed countries. They found no major differences in the status of women in Western countries using their selected criteria (Youssef and Hartley 1979).

Alternatively, Alice Andrews created a status-of-women index using measures of health (life expectancy), education (literacy) and family size (fertility) in a world-wide analysis (Andrews 1982). There are problems with this approach, as she acknowledged an ideal status-of-women index would include more than social dimensions, but the difficulty of finding stable political and economic indicators for all countries led to their exclusion. On a more fundamental level Andrews does not develop an index measuring women's status relative to men in each society, so it is difficult to distinguish between indicators of the status of women and indicators of overall economic development. She found that the highest status-of-woman indexes occur in Western Europe, Anglo-America and Australia whilst the lowest rankings were almost all of Africa, India and Indo-China. In other words, she found that in societies where literacy and longevity are generally high the status of women was high and in affluent countries the index does not make fine distinctions between nations. So we need to build on these approaches to create a more systematic and multifaceted index of sexual equality which will be applicable for developed countries. One of the most comprehensive analytical frameworks to be developed in recent years has been put forward by the United Nations in the report *Compiling Social Indicators on the Situation of Women* (1984a). This suggests that world-wide indicators should be derived from a range of statistics describing economic activities, education and literacy, marital status and households, health and nutrition and political power. Comparable data in these areas are available using different sources such as censuses of population and housing, sample surveys and registration records.

Many of the demographic indicators suggested by the UN guidelines will be applied in this study, but any comprehensive measure of sexual equality needs to take account of cultural factors as well as economic, social and political data. Attitudinal indicators are left out of the UN guidelines because of the difficulty of obtaining standardised comparative measures. Demographic data cannot by itself describe or explain the status of women. Any complete picture needs to take account of both the actual position of women and how attitudes affect this. The social indicators developed in this study will therefore include subjective attitudes towards women as well as objective economic, political and social conditions. Cultural factors are more difficult to measure, but comparisons can be made using sources such as the EuroBarometer surveys of the ten number countries of the European community.

OBJECTIVE ECONOMIC, POLITICAL AND SOCIAL CONDITIONS

If we accept the need for social indicators, what specific measures should be included? In the economic dimension we need to compare women in the paid labour force in full- and part-time jobs to see where they work. We need to look at the full range of their lives, from middle-class women who have got on in executives boardrooms and professional practices to women in typical positions in offices, shops, factories and farms. We need to compare the occupations held by women and men in their pay, positions and prospects. One of the most striking trends in recent years has been the increase in the number of working women in most developed economies. What jobs do they hold? The media often highlight women who are making real breakthroughs into traditional areas, from fire-fighters to managing directors. But the persistence of job-segregation means that the majority are entering the 'pink-collar ghetto' in menial service work, with poor pay and worse prospects. Is this the same in all countries? Too often we use comparative data on middle-class professional women without bringing working-class women into the picture. On this foundation we can start to analyse the distribution of economic rewards—why, for example, in some countries like the United States women in full-time jobs get only 60 per cent of the average male pay-packet while elsewhere they get over 80 per cent. Has equal-pay, affirmative-action and sex-discrimination legislation had any impact? Any comprehensive economic measure of gender equality would also take account of women in poverty, the increasing numbers of single-parent mothers, elderly widows, the unemployed and women in low pay who are dependent upon welfare benefits. How do state services for women vary cross-culturally?

In relation to economic inequalities we need to analyse the social position of women in terms of the family, marriage and education. The position of women within the family and household is often a key to their participation in the larger society. In some countries traditional patterns of family life continue with considerable sex-role segregation while elsewhere divorce and illegitimate births have produced a high proportion of one-parent families and singles living alone. We need to see where abortion, contraception and child-care are widely available and where they are still legally or financially restricted. Any analysis of the social position of women would also have to take account of the educational opportunities open to both sexes, including access to college and sex segregation by subject, since professional qualifications are increasingly necessary for entry to high-status careers.

It is harder to find comparable data on the political position of women but any comprehensive index of sexual equality has to include the significant dimension of public power. In countries like Denmark and the Netherlands there has been a radical change over the last decades in female representation in national parliaments, while in countries such as the United States and Britain only a few women hold such political positions. As well as in parliaments, we need to compare women in other areas of public power, in government, state bureaucracies, the judiciary, public bodies, pressure groups, unions and parties, to see whether there are any systematic factors to explain national differences.

SUBJECTIVE ATTITUDES

Lastly, we need to examine cultural factors to see how attitudes towards sex roles vary in different societies. Where do women and men believe that household tasks and child-care should be shared equally? Where do they feel most strongly that politics should be a masculine world? Where is there most support for the women's movement? Where do the sexes diverge on major political issues and party support? Any comparative analysis of such cultural factors has more limited sources but the EuroBarometer series of surveys in the European Community allows the analysis of attitudinal data from the ten countries of the EEC. The systematic development of this range of social indicators will allow us to start to investigate the dynamics of social change—why in some societies the position of the sexes has changed further and faster than in others. On the basis of this work we will go on, in Chapter 8, to develop a classification of societies into ideal types depending on the degree of objective and subjective gender equality.

THE COMPARISON OF CAPITALIST DEMOCRACIES

The development of this typology on a systematic basis, using accurate and comprehensive social indicators, should increase our understanding of the dynamics of social change. This comparison focuses on capitalist democracies using the 'relative similarity' strategy which aims to neutralise certain economic and political differences in order to allow a clearer analysis of differences in the status of women. This strategy reduces, in so far as possible, the number of interacting variables in the analysis (Dogan and Pelassy 1984; Przeworski and Teune 1970). Since this study is concerned with the question of party influence, comparisons had to be made in societies where there was genuine potential for competition between political parties with diverse ideological views, which is not possible in totalitarian dictatorships, traditional oligarchies and military regimes. The focus on capitalist democracies allows the comparison of Social Democratic governments and different policy initiatives, on equal pay, abortion, child-care or sex discrimination, in a relatively similar environment.

Twenty-four capitalist democracies are included in this analysis, defined as countries in which in recent years there are political rights (such as the right to participate in free and competitive elections) and civil liberties (such as freedom of speech and association), within a developed market economic system. There is considerable agreement amongst scholars as to which countries can conventionally be classified as democracies. In different studies by Dahl (1971), Banks (1971), Butler *et al.* (1981). Bingham Powell (1982) and Lijphart (1984) there was consensus that nineteen of the countries included in this comparison, as shown in the first column of Table 3.1, were continuous democracies since the end of the war. In the second list there are a further four countries which can be seen as interrupted democracies where the regime was seriously suspended or limited for a period, although there has been democratic rule over the last nine years, including France (1958), Greece (1967–74), Portugal (from 1975) and Spain (from 1975). The second list also includes Switzerland, which can only be classified as a democracy since 1971 when women were allowed to vote, despite conventional definitions which do not take account of this criteria.

These twenty-four countries represent four major regions, including Scandinavia, North America, Western Europe and developed economies in the Pacific area. The analysis focuses on the last twenty years as demands for sexual equality have developed with the second-wave women's movement since the early 1960s, and governments have responded with a range of policy initiatives. Statistics for all countries during this period are not complete, but we have enough data through official sources to see broad longitudinal trends from 1960 to 1981. Since the impact of political or environmental variables is cumulative, we need to analyse the dynamics of change over a number of years. A longer time period would be ideal, but in many cases we

Table 3.1: Capitalist democracies

Continuous since 1945	Interrupted or limited
Australia	France
Austria	Greece
Belgium	Portugal
Canada	Spain
Denmark	Switzerland
Finland	
W. Germany	
Iceland	
Ireland	
Israel	
Italy	
Japan	
Luxembourg	
Netherlands	
Norway	
New Zealand	
Sweden	
United Kingdom	
United States	

just do not have reliable comparative information for earlier years.

PARTISAN STRENGTH

To measure partisan strength, as the major independent political variable, parties are classified into four groups: broad left-wing and right-wing categories, then within these into Social Democratic and Christian Democratic sub-categories. The term 'social democratic' is used to describe those parties which avowedly embody socialist ideals whilst working within a framework of representative democracy. For comparison with most previous studies, Social Democratic parties are operationally defined as those which are affiliated to the Socialist International, thereby guaranteeing a certain ideological homogeneity to the group (Hewitt 1977; Jackman 1980; Castles 1982). This narrow definition, however, cannot be taken as a reliable measure of general socialist strength, as it necessarily excludes other parties who have been successful on the left, including the Communists in countries like Italy, Portugal and France. To develop a more general alternative measure of the strength of left-wing parties we will include all self-designated socialist, social democrat, labour or communist groups (Brooks 1983; Dryzek 1978).

As Castles suggests, we need to extend the analysis beyond Socialist parties, for there is evidence that the strength of parties of the right has more decisive influence on policy outputs, through their power to block as much as to initiate legislative change (Castles 1978; Castles and McKinley 1979). It is more difficult to establish clear-cut criteria for inclusion in a general right-wing category, especially with Liberal parties ranging from 'extreme free-market' to 'centrist-reformist' in ideological orientation. This study, however, can build on the eighteen nation classification developed by Castles (1982), supplementing this for the remaining countries by *The International Almanac of Electoral History* (Mackie and Rose 1982), as shown in Table 3.2. Within this category we can identify the last sub-group which might be expected to have a distinctive impact on public policy concerning sexual equality: parties who are affiliated to the Christian Democratic World Union.

For all these groups, partisan strength is measured by the annual average proportion of seats in the national legislature held by major parties from 1960 to 1981, which takes account of the cumulative impact of these parties when in opposition as well as in government. This seems preferable, therefore, to alternative measures of left-wing party strength, including their electoral support (Cameron 1978) or seats in cabinet government. In parliamentary systems, since cabinet participation is generally a function of legislative strength, we would expect these measures to be highly correlated, as indeed is the case (Jackman 1980; Hewitt 1977; Castles 1982). Only major parties are included, that is those with an average of over 5 per cent of legislative seats, since others could not be expected to have a significant role in the policy outcome. Others have used a composite index of left-wing mobilisation, including Social Democratic rule, left-wing Opposition and trade-union strength (Brooks

Table 3.2: Classifcation of major parties

	Right wing	Centre	Left wing
Australia	Liberal/Country Peoples†		Labour*
Austria		Freedom	Socialist*
Belgium	Liberal (PVV/PLP/PRL) Christian Social (CVP/PSC)†	Volksunie	Socialist (BSP/PSB)*
Canada	Conservative	Liberal	New Democrat*
Denmark	Conservative/Progress	Liberal/Radical	Social Democratic*
Finland	Nat. Coalition	Centre/ Swedish People/ Democratic Union	Socialist Peoples Social Democratic*
France	Gaullist/Centre Social Democrats†	Independent/Republican/ Radical/	Socialist* Communist
Germany	Christian Democrats†	Greens/Free Democratic	Social Democratic*
Greece	New Democracy	Union of the Centre	PASOK* Communist (Ext.)
Iceland	Independence	Progressive	Social Democratic* People's Alliance
Ireland	Fine Gael†	Fianna Fail	Labour*
Israel	Herut/Liberal		Labour*
Italy	Christian Democrats†	Liberals	Socialist* Communist Social Democratic*
Japan	Liberal Democrats	Clean Govnt.	Socialists* Democratic Socialists* Communist
Luxembourg	Democratic/Christian Social†		Socialist Workers* Communist Social Democratic

Table 3.2 (Continued)

	Right wing	Centre	Left wing
Netherlands	Liberal	Democrats '66/Catholic People's/Anti-Revolution. Christian Hist.	Labour*
New Zealand	National		Labour
Norway	Conservative	Liberal/Centre/Christian Peoples	Labour*
Portugal	Centre Social Democrats†		Socialist* Communist Social Democratic
Spain	Union of Democratic Centre†		Social Democratic Workers*/Communist
Sweden	Conservative	Centre/Peoples People's/Radical Democrats/Farmers/Independents	Social Democratic*
Switzerland	Catholic Conservatives		Social Democratic*
UK	Conservative		Labour
USA	Republicans	Democrats	

Note: Major parties: over 5% (average) of legislative seats 1960–81
* Affiliated Socialist International
† Affiliated Christian Democratic World Union

Source: Castles (1982); Mackie and Rose (1982); Day and Degenhardt (1980)

1983); however, as there is no self-evident criteria for weighting the items within this index the simpler measure of parliamentary representation seems more widely acceptable.

As we would expect, given our measures, there is a degree of intercorrelation between these political variables, with a particularly strong relationship between the measures for left-wing and Social Democratic strength (r=.83). Both variables are included for comparison in simple bivarate correlations; however, to simplify the final causal models, and to guard against multicollinearity, only the more inclusive left-wing measure is used. The other partisan measures proved to be independent as there was an insignificant association between right-wing and left-wing strength (r=.12) and between the right-wing and Christian Democratic variables (r=.16) (see Table 4.5).

Given the limitations of the data, with a small universe of cases common to this field of research, considerable caution needs to be exercised in interpreting statistical findings. Given the lack of reliable comparable data, most researchers have worked with even fewer countries than the twenty-four in this study. This gives us relatively few cases to determine which differences among the countries may be regarded as the cause or effect of the observed variance (Roberts 1978). As Castles suggests, therefore, we need to search for patterned relationships for a set of policy outputs over time (Castles 1982: 38). In this study we need to establish whether political parties have an effect on a range of independent indicators of sexual equality: economic, social and political. To analyse the effect of variables, simple correlation will be used along with covariance structure analysis (i.e. Lisrel VI). The advantage of Lisrel over alternative approaches such as multiple regression or path analysis is that it allows the reciprocal effects of observed and latent variables to be estimated in a causal model which can be tested for goodness of fit (Joreskog and Sorbom 1983; Saris and Stronkhorst 1984). The results of Lisrel can also be easily interpreted in a non-technical way using path diagrams. The Maximum Likelihood method of estimation will be used, and the main assumptions of the Lisrel approach are linearity and additivity. Given these methodological and conceptual parameters, and the acknowledge need for statistical caution because of the limitations of the data, we can start to analyse whether some societies are more sexually egalitarian than others and, if so, how far this reflects the policy impact of political parties.

4 The Economic Position of Women

The last decades have seen radical changes in most Western societies as increasing numbers of women have left traditional home roles to enter the paid workforce. Does change, as is often assumed, mean progress? We need to see where there have been marked trends towards sexual equality, defined as a 50:50 distribution of economic rewards, prestige and power between women and men. To measure this we need to know whether women have moved towards equality with men in company boardrooms, executive offices and professional positions, or whether they have only increased their numbers in such traditional low-paying, low-status and low-prospect 'pink collar' jobs as secretaries, waitresses and nurses. Have women experienced increased opportunities, or only a 'double burden' of work in the home and office? Developing economic indicators of equality we can see where there has been most change in the position of the sexes over the last twenty years and how far such change is associated with political or environmental factors.

There are two alternative assessments of trends over the last decades. In the pessimistic view, as a result of social change women now have a 'double burden', their traditional roles in the home are unchanged as they continue to do the bulk of the housework while they are also expected to compete with men in the public sphere to bring in a wage. Time-budget studies suggest that in the industrialised world, even with modern facilities, a housewife spends an average of 56 hours a week on domestic work. In Europe as a whole a working woman has, on average, less than half the free time which her husband enjoys (Szalai 1975). Further female activity in feeding, cleaning and maintaining the household is officially invisible, it goes unrecognised in the calculation of GNP despite the essential contribution this work makes to the national economy. In the paid labour force women are confined to a limited range of 'pink-collar' work, typically routine jobs with poor rewards, low prestige and few opportunities for moving up the career ladder. Further, the trends over time in relative earnings and occupational segregation, as Newland suggests, are not necessarily positive for women. A few countries have substantially narrowed the earnings gap, but progress is not universal, 'these cases seem to be more the exception than the rule' (Newland 1979). World-wide, women continue to earn less than three-quarters of the wages earned by men (United Nations 1985b).

In a comparative study in the early 1970s Galenson gives further support to the pessimistic perspective for she found that occupational segregation by sex was a uniform phenomenon:

Conditions affecting women are basically the same all over the West and in Eastern Europe. Women can perform any type of work; somewhere at some time they have done every type of work that men perform. Nevertheless, women typically work in a narrow range of 'women's occupations' rather than across the entire range of occupations. The 'women's occupations' are usually the least skilled and always low paid. (Galenson 1973: 3)

On the basis of anthropological evidence Margaret Mead's conclusions were similar. Whether women and men performed such tasks as cooking, weaving or hoeing varied in different societies, but there was always a division of labour which was seen as natural, and women's work always received lower status and rewards (Mead 1981). Kate Millet supports this view, arguing that no matter the particular activity, what men do will receive higher status, so that men predominate as doctors in the United States, where it is a highly rewarded profession, while women predominate as physicians in the Soviet Union, where the occupation receives lower wages (Millet 1971). Parallels can be drawn with secretarial work in the Victorian period, when it was largely male, and today when it is predominately female. In this view women can change the activities they perform, they can gain entrance to the higher professions, but this will not affect their status as a group, which is derived from their sex not their activities. As Spender points out, just when women think that they have made some break-throughs, the rules change. In Victorian times, when a university qualification in Greek and Latin was seen as essential for positions of influence, it was felt that women could not 'do' languages. Women gained access to college education, predominating in the humanities, whereupon the entry qualifications shifted over the last decades to math-ematics, science and 'high-tech' subjects (Spender 1985: 183).

To support the perspective that inequalities are inevitable, some point to the situation in the United States, where for every hour of work, the average women continues to take home 50 cents for every male dollar, despite the existence for over twenty years of equal-pay and sex-discrimination Acts, a well-organised and assertive women's movement and increasing numbers of women with college qualifications. If we take a longer time span, the position for minority women in the United States has improved somewhat since before the Second World War, but for white women the position is remarkably static; they were paid 61 per cent of white male wages in 1939, the same as their pay almost half a century later (Meehan 1985). As we have seen, conserva-tives such as Goldberg argue that this broad pattern exists cross-culturally, that nowhere have women been successful in competing with men in the arena of company boardrooms and executive offices (Goldberg 1977). Goldberg believes that as a universal law women can never achieve economic equality in the public sphere due to basic physiological differences.

In the pessimistic view other trends since the 1950s have caused the economic position of many women to deterio-rate. The increase in the divorce rates and the break-up of the traditional family have forced increasing numbers of women into poverty, dependent on low-paid jobs and inad-equate welfare services, as discussed in detail in the next chapter. In Scott's prognosis, the situation of women will get worse:

While women throughout the world are increasingly becoming economically responsible for their children, the income gap between men and women is growing. Long-run trends are that job segregation by gender will also increase; so will the gap between women's training and the demands of technology; so will women's share in the 'secondary' (deadend) jobs as opposed to the 'primary' jobs (Scott 1984: x)

In the recession, cuts in social services have their major impact on women, as both the main providers (social workers, nurses, teachers) and beneficiaries (single-parent mothers, elderly) of welfare (Rein 1985).

In addition, the gains which women have made during the 1970s are not secure; changing political and economic conditions threaten many of the women's rights which have been established.

A range of statutes, constitutional conventions, collective agreements and international directives designed to secure improvements in the position of women were passed during the last decades. World-wide the number of countries with equal-pay legislation on their statute books has increased from twenty-eight in 1978 to ninety in 1983 (United Nations 1985a). Over a hundred countries have ratified the International Labour Office Discrimination (Employment and Occupation) Convention since it was passed in 1958. This aims to eliminate any distinction, exclusion or preference on the grounds of sex which impairs equality of opportunity in employment, vocational training or access to particular occupations (ILO 1985; Vogel-Polsky). Without further government commitment to the costs of implementation and enforcement, however, these conventions may prove only symbolic gains.

In a more optimistic perspective some argue that there are signs of gradual progress as women make breakthroughs into traditionally male-dominated fields. Change cannot be expected to be immediate, as it takes time for women who have recently entered management and the professions to work their way up the career ladder. It has been suggested that the static position of average female pay in the United States is due in part to the very success of women at entry-

level positions in business and professional practices
(Meehan 1985: 92). Optimists further argue there has been
a fundamental shift in public attitudes towards working
women since the 1950s. This is reflected in the widespread
introduction of equal-pay and sex-discrimination legislation,
along with related government initiatives on training opportunities and child-care services, which, it is felt, will gradually have an impact on the labour market when
implemented. From this perspective, certain societies have
become significantly more egalitarian over the last decades.
This suggests that patriarchy is not the result of inevitable
physiological sex differences, but of environmental or
political factors, so that there is the potential for change in
all societies. As Ferber and Lowry found in an international
study, there were considerable differences between countries and over time in female labour-force participation,
occupational distribution and earnings. On this basis they
concluded that the economic status of women is not determined by inherent, immutable differences between the sexes
so much as by cultural factors (Ferber and Lowry 1977: 30).

Controversy surrounds how we interpret the nature of
economic change in the position of women, and also how
far such change has been the result of positive government
initiatives. For those who emphasise political variables,
there are a range of direct and indirect policy instruments
which governments can use to improve the economic
position of women, including equal-pay and sex-discrimination legislation, affirmative action, the availability of
child-care facilities, maternity/paternity rights, the tax structure, social-security schemes and training and educational
opportunities. It can be argued that economic inequalities
between women and men have been reduced in some capitalist democracies as a result of public policies introduced
and implemented by Social Democratic governments.
Others are more sceptical about how far policy instruments
have had a major impact on economic change, compared
with the influence of environmental variables including
economic, demographic and cultural trends such as the
growth and structure of the labour market, patterns of
fertility, and attitudes towards working women. We will
explore this debate using systematic comparative measures

to analyse economic differences between women and men over the last twenty years, to consider the affects of environmental or political factors on social change.

ECONOMIC INDICATORS

Indicators measuring economic equality need to be multi-dimensional, given the complexity of female economic roles. Comparative studies often use a limited range of measures such as the proportion of women in the labour force or the ratio of male to female pay. These factors need to be included but they are insufficient by themselves to measure economic rewards and status. A more comprehensive comparison needs to take account of gender differences in at least four dimensions of economic equality: (1) how many women are in paid employment (*labour-force participation*); (2) what sort of income they receive in all sectors and in manufacturing alone (*equal pay*); (3) how far they are restricted to distinct categories of 'women's work' (*horizontal segregation*); (4) how far women are in the most prestigious sorts of careers (*vertical segregation*). Using male:female ratio measures of equality for uniform comparisons we can build a systematic overview of economic equality by developing operational criteria for each of these dimensions.

Some significant factors have had to be excluded from this analysis for lack of reliable data, particularly comparisons of female poverty, unemployment and the division of labour within the household. Studies suggest that unemployment rates are higher for women than men in the majority of Western European and North American countries (United Nations 1982; OECD 1980; Scott 1984), but there are no accurate comparative measures of the ratio of male:female unemployment since countries have not adopted standardised methods of data collection. Household surveys tend to report higher levels of female unemployment than methods which rely upon official registration since women often do not register if they are not thereby eligible for welfare benefits. Nor can we compare the division of labour and rewards within the home, the UNESCO time-budget studies have made progress in this area but there are no standardised measures for all the countries under comparison (see Szalai 1972). Nor do we have any reliable cross-national guides to female poverty. The OECD suggests that poverty can be defined as those with personal incomes below two-thirds the average but reliable comparative income data is only provided for households, not for individuals within sub-groups of the population (OECD 1982; Norris 1984). Official data reflect governmental priorities. There have been recent efforts by agencies such as the United Nations to revise the collection and definition of statistical data to monitor the situation of women, but until these recommendations are implemented we have to work with available sources (United Nations 1984a, 1984b). The selected measures are not intended to describe all aspects of our economic lives but to focus on significant indicators of equality to develop a classificatory overview.

There continue to be problems with comparisons in this area, statistics on the labour force vary according to the way certain groups are classified in different countries, such as unpaid labour in family businesses and farms, or the population of institutions and the armed forces, but with these qualifications in mind we can use data standardised by the International Labour Office (ILO) to compare labour-force participation in Western societies.

WOMEN IN THE LABOUR FORCE

Of course women have always worked, in the care of children and the elderly, the production of food and the maintenance of the household, but unpaid labour has always been invisible in the official statistics. Traditionally, in non-industrialised communities women played a vital economic function in home-based production such as spinning and weaving, but in the West the transfer to factory-based industrial work meant that many women lost this role, particularly in the middle classes. In Western countries one of the most widespread and significant changes since the 1960s has been the major increase in the number of women in the paid labour force, particularly married women with children. In market economies the trends over the last twenty years have resulted in women again forming a substantial proportion of the paid labour force. Over the last twenty years most capitalist democracies have seen a steady growth in female employment, which increased from 29 to 40 per cent of the total labour force by 1981. In other words, recently there were four women in paid employment for every six men. At the same time as women have been increasing in the labour force, male participation has been declining, and it is predicted that these trends will continue into the future. ILO projections suggest that the female labour force will show a higher rate of increase than the male component in all the countries under comparison except Japan until the year 2000 (ILO 1985). In most capitalist democracies, growth has been particularly strong amongst married women, who constituted two-thirds of all employed women by 1981.

These general trends in female employment, however, mask substantial differences between countries. In the 1980s almost half of the official labour force was female in Scandinavia and North America compared with less than a third in Spain, Ireland and the Netherlands (Fig. 4.1). In certain Western societies the growth of employed women over this period was dramatic, their numbers doubled in Canada, Portugal and Norway, but other societies like Switzerland, Germany and Austria were static (Fig. 4.2). At the same time, Japan, Italy and Australia saw a decline in female labour force participation, due in part to changes in the agricultural sector of the economy (Newland 1979).

The contrasts between societies are even more marked if we look at labour-force participation rates by age. In nearly all capitalist democracies about two-thirds of women are in paid jobs in their early twenties, but by middle age there is a divergent pattern. In Scandinavia women continue at work and in some cases the labour-force activity rate even increases (Fig. 4.3). In many middle-range countries like Germany, Britain and France there is a gradual decline over the years as women leave the workforce to have children, although they often return in later years (the 'M' curve).

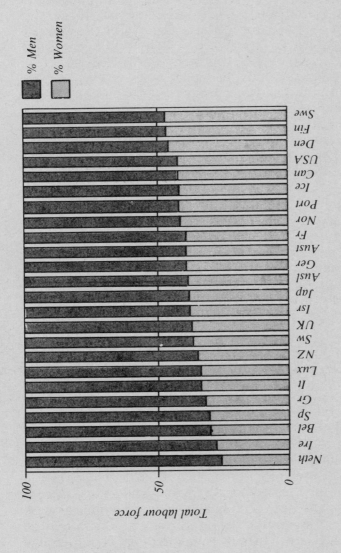

Figure 4.1 : Women in the labour force, 1981

Source: ILO Yearbooks

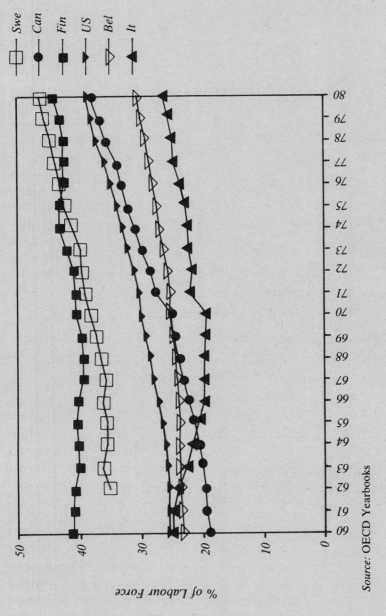

Swe
Can
Fin
US
Bel
It

% of Labour Force

Source: OECD Yearbooks

Figure 4.2 : Growth in female employment, 1960-81

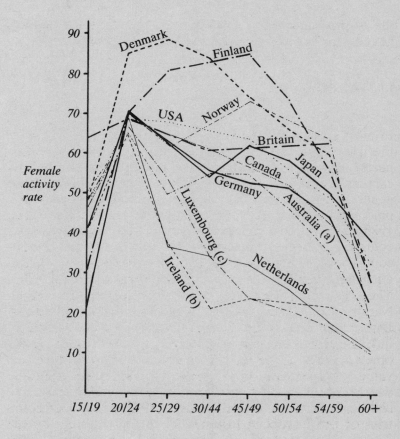

Note: (a) 1976   (b) 1977   (c) 1979

Source: ILO Yearbooks

Figure 4.3 : Female labour-force participation by age, 1981

But in traditional countries like Luxembourg, the Netherlands and Ireland there is a steady decline over the years
until by middle age two-thirds of women are full-time housewives. The net result of these trends is that amongst married
women there are twice as many full-time housewives in

the Netherlands and Ireland (about 80 per cent of married women) as in Denmark and the UK (about 40 per cent).

FEMALE PAY

In most countries more women are in employment than in the late 1950s, but what are their positions, pay and prospects? Has there been a parallel rise in their numbers in careers with high status and earnings? Previous studies have generally stressed that overall women predominate in poorly paid and low-status jobs, but it can be suggested that by the 1980s this was not a uniform tendency as there are significant conrasts between societies. All the countries under comparison have ratified the ILO Convention (No. 100) on equal remuneration for work of equal value (Flanz 1983). These countries have also been signatories to the United Nations Convention on the Elimination of All Forms of Discrimination Against Women (1979), which in Article 11 includes rights for women to work, to equal employment opportunities, to equal remuneration for work of equal value, to promotion, to job security, to social security, and which encourages the introduction of maternity leave and child-care services (United Nations 1985b). Member countries of the European Community are also bound by the Treaty of Rome and EC Directives to implement equal pay (1962), equal worth (1975) and equal treatment in job promotions and recruitment (1976) (see Warner 1984). Individual countries have also introduced a range of equal-pay and opportunity policies involving collective agreements between trade unions and employers (Sweden, Belgium); litigation within law (United States, Canada, France); administrative enforcement within the law (Britain, France); and training and educational programmes (Austria, Sweden) (see OECD 1980, 1985; European Commission 1983; Vogel-Polsky 1985).

Given this range of policy initiatives, how far have pay differentials diminished over the last twenty years? There are alternative criteria to compare the ratio of male to female pay, such as monthly, weekly or hourly wages; gross pay or take home pay inclusive of overtime and tax. Comparisons can be drawn for part-time or full-time workers, and those in agricultural, manufacturing or the service sectors of the economy. Full-time hourly pay in all sectors except agriculture is the most straightforward comparative measure as it excludes national differences in the length of the working week for men and women and the problems of defining part-time work and agricultural payments in kind. Hourly pay, including overtime, bonuses and special premiums, provides a conservative estimate. As women tend to work less hours per week an analysis of take-home pay would show greater inequalities between the sexes. To supplement this we will also compare full-time hourly pay in the manufacturing sector alone, to provide a measure of working-class as well as middle-class pay.

These comparisons of average pay show that the male: female pay differential varies substantially between countries (Fig. 4.4). In Japan, the most unequal society, women receive only half of the average male wage in all sectors of the economy and this has remained largely unchanged in recent decades. The inequalities in countries such as the United States and Ireland have also remained static over the years. In contrast, women in Australia, Denmark and France now earn over 80 per cent of average male hourly pay and there have been clear trends towards greater economic equality. In many countries the gradual improvements in female pay during the 1960s were accelerated during the 1970s despite the recession. In capitalist democracies average hourly pay for women steadily increased from 63 per cent of male wages in 1961 to 77 per cent in 1983. Cross-cultural contrasts were even stronger in the manufacturing sector of the economy, where women received relatively high pay (80 to 90 per cent of male wages) in the Nordic countries and Australia compared with less than half (43 per cent) of male wages in Japan.

How do we explain these cross-cultural contrasts? Wage differentials represent a complex phenomenon but two immediate causes are commonly suggested: horizontal and vertical segregation. With horizontal segregation women are limited to certain areas of employment, in factories as sewers not welders, or in schools as nursery not secondary-

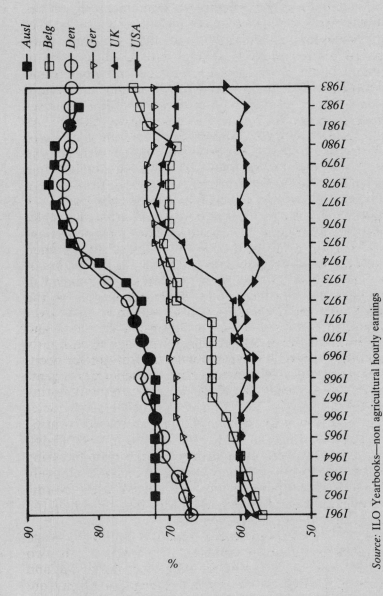

Source: ILO Yearbooks—non agricultural hourly earnings

Figure 4.4 : Ratio of male to female pay, 1961–83

school teachers. With vertical segregation the most prestigious and well-paid professional and managerial careers are dominated by men. Before we can analyse the impact of equal-pay policies we therefore need to outline how far occupational segregation varies by country and over time.

HORIZONTAL SEGREGATION

To see how far women are confined to a restricted range of occupations we need a comparative analysis of sex segregation in a range of occupational categories, in factories, offices and shops. The labour market is divided into segments which are largely self-contained as there is little mobility for workers to transfer to different sectors. In Western Europe and North America there are a number of occupations where women predominate; they constitute 92 per cent of secretaries and typists in these countries, 88 per cent of nurses and midwives, 92 per cent of housekeepers and maids, and 80 per cent of charworkers and cleaners (United Nations 1980). This segregation is of importance because the labour market segments in which women are concentrated tend to be disadvantaged in terms of skill, status, security and earnings; indeed, they tend to form a 'secondary labour market'.

To analyse this more systematically we can develop a comparative segregation index using the major (one digit) ISCO occupational groups. It would have been preferable to analyse segregation in more detailed occupational groups—for example, breaking down the professional group into medical workers, then subdividing into physicians, technicians and nurses—but comparative sex-segregated data is not available at the two-digit and three-digit classification level. In interpreting the results it should be noted that an analysis restricted to the major occupational groups is likely to produce a conservative estimate of segregation (OECD 1985: 48). The degree of segregation, following OECD practice, is measured as the relationship between the proportion of women in the occupation and the proportion of women in the labour force (OECD 1985: 40). This can be expressed as a coefficient of female representation (CFR), where unity (1.00) implies that the female share of an occupational group is the same as the female share in total employment. In other words, if in a society women form 40 per cent of the workforce and 40 per cent of teachers, then the coefficient will equal unity (1.00). In the same society, if only 12 per cent of lawyers are women then female underrepresentation will be expressed with a coefficient less than unity (0.30). Alternatively, if women are overrepresented, if they constitute 78 per cent of secretaries, then the coefficient would be more than unity (1.95). Using these coefficients allows comparisons between countries over the last decades, separating segregation from other factors such as growth in the female workforce.

Using these measures, certain trends in occupational segregation are apparent. Women are still entering areas of 'women's work', but there has been a gradual decline in job segregation in most sectors, confirmed in other studies (OECD 1985: 54). In 1981 women were most strongly over-represented in service (1.80) and clerical (1.64) occupations, including such jobs as cooks, waitresses, cleaners, hair-dressers, bookkeepers and typists. Women are also overrepresented, although to a lesser extent, in the professional (1.21) and sales (1.27) groups (Fig. 4.5). Changes over the last decades have produced a decrease in occupational segregation, but this needs to be carefully interpreted. The main shift has come from men entering 'women's work', in the expanding service and professional sectors, rather than women breaking through into 'men's work' in management and the factory floor, a trend noted in other studies (Hakim 1979; Liljestrom 1984). In 1960 women were most strongly underrepresented in the administrative sector (.36), and the average position had not changed twenty years later. In manufacturing, segregation even increased from 1960 (.51) to 1981 (.41), it can be suggested partly due to the cutbacks in production.

As we would expect, however, occupational segregation varies substantially between societies (Table 4.1). Female underrepresentation in administrative and managerial jobs, for example, ranged from .10 in Spain and .15 in Switzerland

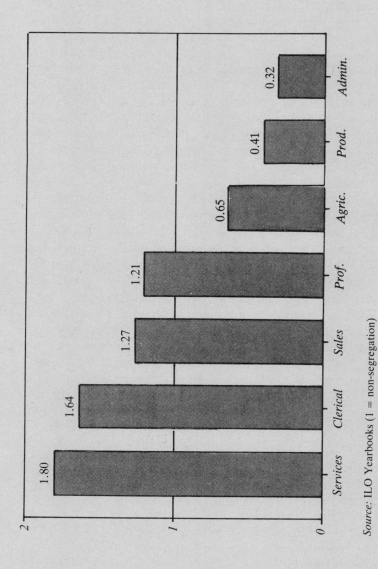

Source: ILO Yearbooks (1 = non-segregation)

Figure 4.5 : Occupational segregation, 1981

Table 4.1: Comparative occupational segregation, 1981

	Female over representation					Female under representation			
	Service	Cler.	Sales	Prof.	*Av.*	Agric.	Prod.	Admin.	*Av.*[a]
Australia	1.60	1.82	1.32	1.22	1.49	0.67	0.32	0.65	0.49
Austria	1.87	1.55	1.51	1.19	1.53	1.24	0.38	0.35	0.37
Belgium	2.11	1.58	1.70	1.49	1.72	0.57	0.53	0.35	0.44
Canada	1.32	1.90	0.98	1.26	1.37	0.50	0.34	0.75	0.55
Denmark	1.28	1.63	1.31	1.35	1.39	0.32	0.40	0.38	0.39
Finland	1.69	1.83	1.23	1.17	1.48	0.86	0.46	0.35	0.41
W. Ger.	1.46	1.55	1.48	1.02	1.38	1.23	0.40	0.44	0.42
Greece	1.33	1.46	1.94	1.10	1.21	1.28	0.49	0.33	0.41
Ireland	2.02	2.55	1.24	1.65	1.87	0.32	0.46	0.44	0.45
Israel	1.48	1.68	0.81	1.41	1.35	0.37	0.30	0.31	0.31
Japan	1.45	1.44	1.04	1.18	1.28	1.26	0.68	0.18	0.43
Lux.	2.24	1.39	1.74	1.09	1.62	0.98	0.16	0.16	0.16
Neth.	2.47	1.66	1.40	1.32	1.71	0.57	0.22	0.26	0.24
Norway	1.86	1.88	1.41	1.31	1.62	0.61	0.35	0.41	0.38
NZ	1.54	2.01	1.19	1.28	1.51	0.60	0.43	0.24	0.34
Portugal	1.66	1.20	1.04	1.30	1.30	1.25	0.57	0.32	0.45
Spain	1.92	1.31	1.40	1.28	1.48	0.86	0.42	0.10	0.26
Sweden	1.62	1.74	1.00	1.16	1.38	0.50	0.38	0.43	0.41
Switz.	1.85	1.46	1.55	1.05	1.48	0.73	0.39	0.15	0.27
UK	1.90	1.65	1.30	1.05	1.48	0.36	0.47	0.23	0.35
USA	1.40	1.83	1.14	1.14	1.38	0.34	0.46	0.72	0.59
Average	1.80	1.64	1.27	1.21	1.48	0.65	0.41	0.32	0.38

Notes: (a) Average production and administration only
Source: ILO Yearbooks

to .75 in Canada. For an overall comparison we can develop two summary measures for those occupations where women are underrepresented in administration and production (excluding agriculture due to the problems of reliable data) and overrepresented in clerical, service, sales and professions. The results in Table 4.1 suggest that the highest degree of occupational segregation by sex exists in the Netherlands, with Canada and the USA as the most integrated economies. Horizontal segregation partially explains the pay differentials between male and female wages: due to tradition, cultural attitudes, educational qualifications and training opportunities, women continue to enter 'women's work', which is often poorly rewarded. As important as the horizontal division of labour, however, is vertical segregation by sex. Even within broad occupational groups, women predominate as junior lecturers not heads of department, shop assistants not managers, general practitioners not senior consultants. To compare how far women are making breakthroughs into the higher levels of management and the professions we can use measures of economic status.

OCCUPATIONAL PRESTIGE AND VERTICAL SEGREGATION

Considerable research has gone into developing indices of occupational prestige, ranking different jobs along a single hierarchy, due to the centrality of this concept for the analysis of social class (Duncan 1961; Featherman and Hauser 1975; Treiman 1977; Powers 1982). The prestige of workers, whether miners, nurses, bank managers, teachers or nuclear physicists, varies according to the amount of deference, regard, honour and respect given to these jobs. We gain prestige through various activities, of which our occupation is one of the most important (Shils 1968: 107–8). Prestige is measured by asking a sample of respondents to rank a set of occupational titles in terms of their social standing. On the basis of this research, a comparison by Treiman (1977) of over sixty countries concluded that societies are similar in terms of the relative prestige awarded occupations. He found that occupations are ranked in a similar order in all countries, with the most prestige given to higher management and certain professions such as medical practitioners, architects and college professors.

There is general agreement throughout the world in the hierarchical ordering of occupations. A single prestige dimension appears to underlie the observed prestige hierarchy in every society. . . . On the average, people in all walks of life, rich and poor, educated and ignorant, urban and rural, male and female, view the prestige hierarchy in the same way. With minor exceptions, there is extraordinary consensus throughout each society regarding the relative prestige of occupations (Treiman 1977: 59)

Further, the relative prestige of occupations are fairly stable over time, with no major differences between industrialised and non-industrialised countries (Inkeles and Rossi 1956) nor between sub-groups of the population. Not only do women evaluate occupations in the same way men do, identifying the sex of the incumbent makes no difference in the prestige accorded occupations (Treiman 1977: 212).

Whilst the professions are ranked highest in status, most previous comparisons which include all jobs within this category are not very reliable since this includes a wide range of groups, nurses as well as doctors, nursery teachers as well as university professors, in the International Standards Classification of Occupations (ISCO-1968). Within this broad category, therefore, we need to compare selected occupations which are highest in prestige.

Using the prestige scale developed by Treiman (1977), designed to provide a valid comparison for all capitalist democracies, we can rank occupations in a scale between 0 and 100 to see how far women have achieved equality in the most prestigious jobs. The groups of jobs which ranked amongst the highest in status included university and college teachers (rank scale 78), physical and life scientists (66), medical physicians, dentists, veterinarians and pharmacists (60), architects, engineers and related technicians (56) and administrative and managerial workers (64). In contrast at the bottom of the scale there are a number of occupations, both those which are predominately male such as garbage collectors (13) and unskilled construction labourers (15), as well as those predominately female such as hotel chambermaids (14) and charworkers (16). The main comparisons in the male:female ratio in the most prestigious professions are given in Table 4.2.

As Table 4.2 shows, women were in a minority in all the most prestigious occupations. In capitalist democracies women constituted, on average, 12 per cent of architects and engineers, 37 per cent of physical and life scientists, 33 per cent of medical doctors, pharmacists and dentists, 36 per cent of university teachers and 18 per cent of managers (United Nations 1980). This has been widely recognised in previous studies. What is less often emphasised is the considerable variation by country; there were more women than men amongst scientists and related technicians in France, Greece, the Netherlands and Norway, whilst women predominated amongst medical professionals in

Table 4.2: Women in selected professions, 1970 (% of women)

	Eng./Ar. (i)	Admin. (ii)	Teaching (iii)	Science (iv)	Medical (v)	Average (i–v)
Austria	10.6	28.6	. . .	37.5	35.7	28.1
Belgium	19.4	20.5	50.0	33.3	33.3	31,3
Canada	5.7	23.6	40.0	23.1	18.2	22.1
Denmark	18.4	12.4	25.0	82.4	35.7	32.8
Finland	3.4	13.2	25.0	33.3	64.3	27.8
France	11.2	20.3	50.0	58.3	38.5	35.7
Greece	42.9	26.3	. . .	57.1	. . .	42.1
W. Germany	7.2	23.4	33.3	46.2	43.8	30.8
Ireland	6.7	8.8	33.3	20.0	33.3	20.4
Italy	11.1	20.0	50.0	33.3	30.8	29.0
Netherland	2.2	12.8	. . .	52.2	. . .	22.4
Norway	8.3	15.6	25.0	50.0	38.5	27.5
Portugal	12.5	11.1	. . .	12.5	. . .	12.0
Spain	10.5	14.3	. . .	. . .	. . .	12.4
Sweden	12.0	22.7	25.0	28.6	41.7	26.0
Switz.	16.7	9.1	. . .	16.7	27.3	17.4
UK	15.1	14.3	. . .	20.0	33.3	20.7
USA	7.5	21.1	38.5	22.2	18.2	21.5
Average	12.3	17.7	35.9	36.9	35.2	25.6

Note: (i) Architects, engineers and related technicians
       (ii) Administrative and managerial
       (iii) University and higher-education teachers
       (iv) Physical and life scientsts
       (v) Medical doctors, dentists, veterinarians, pharmacists.
Source: United Nations (1980)

Finland. Relative differences by country are considerable in
each category; for instance, only 2 per cent of engineers
and architects are women in the Netherlands, while they
form almost 20 per cent in Denmark and Belgium. The
proportion of women in administration and management
shows again wide variation between countries: about a third
of managers are female in North America while there are
very few (less than 6 per cent) in countries such as Japan,
the Netherlands and Switzerland.

Given educational trends, there is some evidence that the
number of professional women may gradually increase in the
future. Growing numbers of women are entering universities
and technical institutes; almost half of all college students
are women in the United States, Canada, Denmark,
Finland, France and West Germany. This represents a

marked change since the 1960s as the average proportion of women at college has risen in all these countries from 29 to 43 per cent of students in 1981, as we will discuss in detail in the next chapter. More women are graduating; however, sex segregation persists in the sort of qualifications they are obtaining as women still tend to study in the humanities, fine arts and education faculties. In recent years women continue to be a minority of students in professional fields where men have traditionally dominated; on average they constitute 34 per cent of students in law, 27 per cent in mathematics and computer science, 22 per cent in architecture and town planning, 31 per cent in business and commerce and only 7 per cent in engineering (UNESCO 1984). This varies by country; there is greater sex equality in these fields in Finland, France and Sweden, but all countries are characterised by sex segregation by subject. If female graduates in professional and business subjects break through into the workforce in these fields, this should gradually lead to a more egalitarian labour market, although formal qualifications are only the first hurdle in high-status careers.

It might have been expected that those countries with a high proportion of women in administrative, managerial and professional jobs would have correspondingly high average female wages, but this is not necessarily the case. The United States and Canada, for example, both have more women in these prestigious occupations than Australia, yet they have much lower average wages. A simple correlation between the indicators for pay and occupational prestige show only a weak association ($r = .23$). This can be explained by analysing the distribution of female earnings among different classes. Middle-class women are relatively successful in getting ahead in boardrooms and executive offices in the United States, yet the vast majority of American women are entering poorly paid jobs as typists and clerks, cashiers, restaurant waitresses, office cleaners and factory assemblers. In contrast, in Australia and Italy there are relatively few women in the most prestigious jobs, but the pay for working-class women is higher, which raises the overall average.

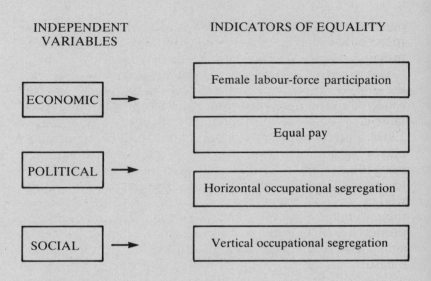

Figure 4.6 : Theoretical model of economic equality

EXPLANATIONS OF ECONOMIC EQUALITY

The significance of these indicators of economic equality can only be seen if we move from the description to the analysis of cross-cultural differences. Within our framework of the policy output model a number of environmental and political factors can be suggested to explain cross-cultural variations in economic equality (Fig. 4.6). In the *environmental* category economic factors, including the level of economic development and the growth of the economy, could be expected to affect the *demand* for female workers. Previous studies have emphasised that women's labour-force participation is largely a consequence of economic development (OECD 1980; Collver and Langlois 1962; Wilensky 1968; Klein 1963; Semyonov 1980; Oppenheimer 1973). In this view, industrialisation brings women to the work place through changes in the occupational structure, especially the growth in service and white-collar work, coupled with increased educational opportunities. To analyse the effects of the level of economic development this is measured as per capita GNP (dollars) in 1981, while economic growth is represented by the change in GNP per capita over the previous twenty years (World Bank 1983a).

It has been suggested that social variables also influence the *supply* of women workers, including family patterns reflected in the rates for fertility and the proportion of non-married women in the population (Collver and Langlois 1962). Patterns of family organisation could be expected to play a significant role in the economic position of women, since the decline in fertility gives women more opportunities to participate, while patterns of family instability may force women to join the workforce to support themselves and their children. Rather than the crude divorce rate, the proportion of non-married women in the female working-age population was included, as this is a more inclusive measure of the number of women (divorced, single or widowed) who may have to work to support themselves (UN Demographic Yearbook 1984).

Lastly, educational qualifications may be influential in labour-force participation and pay. Many economists argue that the demand for workers, and therefore the rewards which they receive in the labour market, depends on their 'human capital', that is their training, education and experience (Stevenson 1978). If women invest less in their 'human capital' than men, then they will be paid lower wages. To analyse this relationship educational qualifications will be included in the analysis, measured as the ratio of women to men in university and higher education (UNESCO 1984).

The supply and demand for women in the job market is one of the primary explanations for their economic rewards for economists in the neoclassical school (see Sweet 1973; Berch 1982). If the structure of the economy changes so that there is increased demand for the skills and experience which women bring to the job market—for example by a shift from heavy manual labouring to white-collar clerical work—then it is argued that in a situation of perfect competition the wage rates for women will rise to attract them into the labour force. In its simplest form, neoclassical economists assume that the decision to enter the workforce is one aspect of consumer choice. Women are faced with a choice between leisure, work and the consumption of goods

and services. The choice is made in the context of inter-
vening variables, including facilitating conditions such as
the woman's education and experience, enabling conditions
such as the number and age of any children in the household, and precipitating conditions including the financial
circumstances of the household and social attitudes towards
work. Given this model women will enter the workforce if
wage rates are sufficiently attractive to make work preferable to leisure, and the employer will offer sufficient wage
rates to meet the demand for labour (Sweet 1973; Berch
1982).

Lastly, there are *political* variables since governments can
affect the role of women in the labour market by a range
of public policies. These include policies concerning the
availability of child-care facilities, maternity/paternity
leave, the tax structure, social-security schemes, in addition
to specific legislation on equal pay, equal worth, affirmative
action, sex discrimination and protective restrictions. To
promote equal opportunities, governments can also create
administrative bodies to advise on women's rights, use
public-information campaigns and positive quota systems to
stimulate female access to jobs traditionally held by men.
Governments may also affect women in the labour force
through a range of more indirect measures, such as regu-
lations on minimum wages, policies on migration, the
provision of social services, and training schemes to alleviate
unemployment (OECD 1980). These are indirect instruments as the intention is not necessarily to benefit women
as such; for example, minimum-wage standards are designed
for all workers, but since women are amongst the lowest
paid they are amongst the main beneficiaries. Again, the
expansion or contraction of social services has an impact on
all workers in these fields, but as a result this largely affects
women as social-workers, teachers and nurses (Rein 1985).
The argument is therefore that we would expect political
parties to have an impact on sexual equality through both
direct and indirect measures, with left-wing and Social
Democratic governments improving the position of women
in accordance with their more interventionist and egalitarian
ideology.

CONCLUSIONS

To analyse the influence of political and environmental factors on economic equality these factors were entered into a single causal model using covariance structure analysis (Lisrel). The results of this analysis, including only statistically significant relationships (p= > 0.05) are summarised in Figure 4.7. From this we can conclude that political parties have little impact on female labour-force participation, which was affected primarily by levels of economic development and female education. Together these factors explained 64 per cent of variance, confirming the results of previous studies (Collver and Langlois 1962; Wilensky 1968; Klein 1963; Semyonov 1980). In post-industrial societies, therefore, it seems that economic development changes the occupational structure. There is an expansion of opportunities for women in the service sector and white-collar office work but a decline in traditional male jobs in manufacturing and heavy industry. In addition, educational trends increase the supply of women with the qualifications and experience required by employers. Other factors which might affect female participation, including patterns of marriage and the family, proved insignificant.

Although political parties have no direct influence on female labour-force participation, they have had a major impact on female pay and positions. The results of this analysis suggests that Socialist governments have achieved a substantive impact on reducing pay differentials ($\gamma = .65$) through a range of direct and indirect measures, including legislation on equal pay and sex discrimination as well as policies such as minimum-wage standards. This implies that the extensive range of initiatives introduced during the 1970s were not merely symbolic, as they have had a major influence, as others have found (OECD 1985). Through these policies left-wing parties have also achieved a significant reduction in occupational segregation, both horizontal ($\gamma = -.56$) and vertical ($\gamma = -.38$). In contrast, right-wing party strength was significantly associated with increased levels of horizontal ($\gamma = .45$) and vertical ($\gamma = .65$) segregation. Environmental factors were also found to

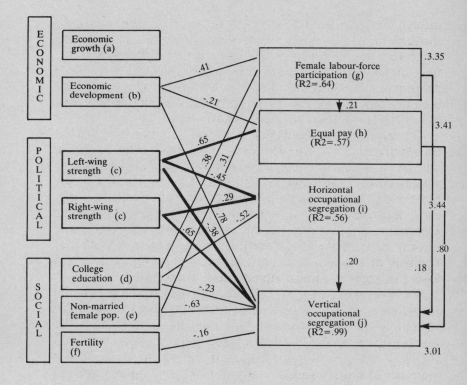

Notes and sources: The estimates are based on Lisrel Maximum Likelihood Coefficients. Only statistically significant relationships are reported (p. = >0.05). (a) Growth in GNP per capita 1960-81 (World Bank 1983a).(b) GNP per capita 1981 (World Bank 1983a). (c) Average percentage of seats held by parties 1960-81 (Mackie and Rose 1984). (d) Percentage of male to female students in third-level education 1981 (UNESCO 1984). (e) Percentage of working-age female population, single, widowed, divorced or never married 1981 (*UN Demographic Yearbook* 1984). (f) Fertility rate, 1981 (*UN Demographic Yearbook* 1984). (g) Ratio of male to female labour force participation, 1981 (*ILO Yearbook of Labour Statistics* 1960-84). (h) Ratio of male to female full-time hourly pay *c.* 1981 (*ILO Yearbooks*). (i) Males to females selected sectors 1981, see text for details, p.65 (*ILO Yearbooks*). (j) Males to females in selected professions 1979, see text for details, p.68 (United Nations 1980).

Figure 4.7 : Causal model of economic equality

influence occupational segregation; women are breaking through into the higher professional careers in societies where economic development has expanded the opportunities in these occupations and where there are a high proportion of non-married and well-educated women, which is to be expected given that entry into the higher professions is largely restricted to college graduates.

Therefore, two general conclusions can be drawn from this analysis. First, the economic position of women varies widely between democratic capitalist states: patterns of sexual stratification are far from universal. While women have not achieved absolute equality in any capitalist democracy, there are marked contrasts between such societies as Denmark and Ireland, or Australia and the Netherlands. On the basis of these systematic comparisons it is clear that the role of women in employment has changed further and faster in some capitalist democracies than others.

Second, while social and economic variables set the parameters within which governments operate, we can conclude that environmental variables do not determine the position of working women. Socialist parties have reduced the pay differential and occupational segregation facing women, although still not as far as many feminist would desire. Politics *does* matter, compared with other factors such as the level of economic development or economic growth. This has significant implications for active feminists; it suggests that working within organised socialism can be an effective route to achieve the economic goals of the women's movement. If we accept that governments have an impact in the economic sphere, the question remains, however, whether they have equal influence in the social sphere, on matters of crucial importance to women such as child-care, abortion and education? Or are these bipartisan issues, cutting across the traditional left–right political dimension. Therefore we need to consider the relationship between political parties and the social position of women.

5 The Social Position of Women

To transform the conditions of reproduction as well as production many of the primary goals of the women's movement revolve around issues of sexuality, marriage and the family, as well as those of education and health. Even if the conditions of women's paid employment were to improve, they would still face a double burden unless we simultaneously transform social lives in the family and personal relationships. Legal changes concerning equal pay and sex discrimination can only have a limited impact; they may help women break through into high-powered professional and executive careers, but unless sex roles in the family and socail institutions also change, all that women will have achieved is to double their workload, in the home and office. Early studies explaining sex differences in employment often stressed factors in the labour market, such as female qualifications or employer discrimination, in isolation from the family lives of women. In contrast, more recent theorists argue that, given the double burden facing most women, we can only understand economic inequalities, such as why more women enter the lower-paid part-time sector, in the context of our social lives. This chapter aims is to see where there has been most change in the social position of the sexes over the last twenty years, using comparative indicators, and how far such change is associated with political or environmental variables.

Public policies influence the institutional context of the family in many respects, including the legal status of marriage; civic divorce, property rights and the custody of dependents; welfare benefits and household taxes;

maternity, child-care and schooling facilities; services for the elderly; and violence within the home. The law also has a major impact on the control of sexuality within society, including restrictions on contraception, abortion, incest, child sexual abuse, pornography, prostitution, rape and rights for homosexuals. In our everyday lives the law sets the parameters to what is considered 'normal', for example in sexual relations or the care of children. Through public policy, therefore, we would expect that the state could have a major impact on facilitating or restricting social change in the lives of women and men.

FEMINIST GOALS

Given the complexities of public policy in this area, this chapter will focus on comparative social indicators in four specific areas which have been central to feminist demands: educational opportunities, abortion rights, maternity services and child-care facilities. Each of these areas represents different aspects of women's social lives with significant implications for sexual equality. As a result, the women's movement has raised these issues as matters of urgent concern for the policy-making agenda. The women's movement has different priorities and strategies in each country, depending upon circumstances, but most share a set of common concerns. Feminists argue that women will not have control over their own lives until they have control over the reproductive and childrearing process, through making abortion, contraception and child-care facilities a matter of choice. One of the primary goals of the women's movement has been to make abortion legally available in all circumstances, with the decision resting with the women concerned rather than medical practitioners or other author-ities. Women have also been working to gain improvements in the maternity services, to make childbirth a safer and more rewarding experience, where the mother has more control over the process. The growth in the numbers of one-parent families and working women has led to the increased need for child-care services provided by the state, including crèches, nursery schools and kindergartens. Lastly, education has long been seen as the key for the transformation of social attitudes and opportunities. Unless women have equal access to formal qualifications, they will be automatically excluded from the most prestigious, powerful and highly rewarded positions in society. Access by itself is insufficient, however, since the curricula, methods of research and even the functions of university education need to be altered to take account of the feminist perspective.

ASSESSMENT OF TRENDS

Over the last decades there have been significant changes in women's social lives, but how we interpret these trends is open to dispute. On the one hand, there have been clear feminist gains: in many countries some of the most striking breakthroughs have been in educational opportunities. Increasing numbers of women are entering university; today women constitute over half of all graduates in Canada, Israel and the United States. Sex segregation by subject conttnues, but more women areegaininqualifications which lead to well-paid careers in fields traditionlly dominated by men, such as laww medicine and business.

The issue of reproductive rights has caused stronger public controversy in most countries. There has been a recent world-wide trend to relax the laws on abortion; from the late 1960s until 1982 over forty countries extended their grounds and only three narrowed them. This change has meant that world-wide nearly two-thirds of women now live in countries where laws permit abortion on request or in a wide variety of circumstances. Less than one in ten live in countries where abortion is totally prohibited (Francome 1984). As a result, it is estimated that there are around 50 million induced abortions a year (Tietz 1979). The law on abortion varies considerably in different societies, in such matters as the time limits for abortion, the accepted grounds to qualify and the degree of state funding of abortion services. By 1985 women had legal access to abortion in all countries under comparison except for Ireland, Belgium and

Spain (United Nations 1982). Reproductive choice has also been increased by the wider availability of birth-control devices, so that by 1981 about three-quarters of married women were using contraceptives in capitalist democracies (United Nations 1985). Maternity/parental leave and child-care facilities have been expanded, and there has also been increased public recognition of the need to deal with violence against women, with the foundation of a network of battered women and rape-crisis shelters, often with government financial support.

On the other hand there is a more pessimistic overall assessment. Although more women are now in college, they are still a minority in those subjects which are likely to provide many of the expanding technological jobs in the 1980s, including computer studies, electronic engineering and physical science. In addition, as Adrienne Rich points out, it has also proved easier for women to succeed educationally in traditional subjects than to achieve a significant transformation of the mainstream curricula (Rich 1980).

Although there have also been improvements over the last decades in the area of reproductive rights, in few countries have feminists achieved abortion on demand, as a matter of the woman's choice (Francome 1984). Recent reforms have also been threatened by the growth of the New Right and the development of influential groups such as the Moral Majority in the United States. Many countries have also seen an expansion of child-care facilities, with state-run nurseries, crèches and kindergartens for pre-school children. This expansion, however, has not necessarily kept pace with the additional demand for these services, given the growth in working mothers and single-parent families.

THE FEMINISATION OF POVERTY

Positive reforms over the last decades have to be set in the context of widespread changes in family life. The rising divorce and illegitimacy rate in many countries has led to the increased feminisation of poverty, with growing numbers of single-parent mothers dependent on welfare and low rates of pay. This phenomenon has been particularly noted in the United States, where today two out of three of the adult poor are women (Kamerman 1984). Half of all poor children live in female-headed one-parent families (Congress 1985). Further, the trend is escalating with female-headed households the fastest growing type of family in the country (Stallard, Ehrenreich and Sklar 1983). In the decade since the mid-1960s the number of poor adult American males declined, while according to official definitions the number of poor women-headed families increased by 100,000 a year (Ehrenreich and Stallard 1982; Pearce 1979; Schfran 1982; Sawhill 1976; Norris 1984). This situation has been compounded in the United States since the early 1970s by the failure of welfare benefits to rise in line with inflation (Congress 1985).

Nor is the feminisation of poverty confined to the developed world. There is a cross-cultural trend towards increasing rates of divorce, migration and family instability, with the result that world-wide between a quarter and a third of all families are supported by women and therefore vulnerable to poverty and hardship (Newland 1979; Scott 1984). In Third World societies female-headed households are a growing phenomenon; for example, in Africa women head 40 per cent of households in Kenya, Ghana and Sierra Leone (United Nations 1985a). If the feminisation of poverty is an increasing trend throughout the world it can be suggested that over the last decades, while women have won the battle, with clear policy gains concerning equal rights, in many ways they have lost the war.

How far are trends towards the decline of the traditional family apparent cross-culturally? The increase in divorce has been evident in most countries, with a moderate rise in the 1960s followed by dramatic growth in the early 1970s (Fig. 5.1). The average divorce rate doubled over the last decades although the rate varies substantially between societies.[1] By 1985 civil divorce had been liberalised in all capitalist democracies except Ireland, although it was only recently legalised in Italy (1971) and Spain (1981) and made easily available in Greece (1983) and Portugal (1975). The divorce rate continues to be relatively low in these latter

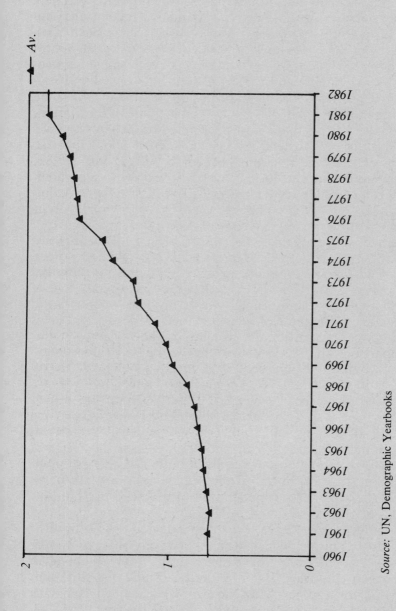

Source: UN, Demographic Yearbooks

Figure 5.1 : Divorce trends in capitalist democracies, per 1,000 population 1960-82

countries, along with Japan and Israel. At the other extreme, the divorce rate is highest in the United States, followed by countries sharing an Anglo-American or Scandinavian cultural heritage. These divorce trends have significant consequences for the growth of single-parent families, since in 1981 two-thirds of divorcing couples had dependent children (United Nations 1984a).

The divorce rate is one indicator of the breakdown of the traditional family but it is not a reliable guide to the number of single women in society since rates of remarriage vary cross-culturally. Instead, we need a direct comparison of the proportion of non-married women in the population, including in this category all who are widowed, separated, divorced or single (never-married). Within capitalist democracies we need to compare the working-age female population (20–59 years) to control for differential rates of longevity and childbirth. The results of this comparison are striking: in 1981 between a quarter and a third of all women were non-married, with the highest rates in the Nordic countries (Fig. 5.3). This suggests that the traditional view of women in the family unit, with a husband supporting a dependent wife and children, no longer applies to the lives of a large proportion of women in the societies under comparison. In 1981 amongst the working-age population most women (72 per cent) were married but a further 19 per cent were single (never-married), while a few were widowed (4 per cent), divorced (5 per cent) and separated (3 per cent). To some extent this trend reflects the rising number of couples who are living together without the legal formalities of marriage but household census data suggest that cohabitation only accounts for part of this phenomenon. In addition in the whole population only half of all females are married, which is often overlooked in generalisations about the status of women.

Family patterns have also been affected by the rate of illegitimate births, which has dramatically increased over the last two decades, on average more than doubling in European countries. By 1982 the percentage of all babies born out of wedlock had reached 38 per cent in Denmark and 14 per cent in France and Britain (EuroStat 1984: 55). These trends in the divorce and illegitimacy rates have inevi-

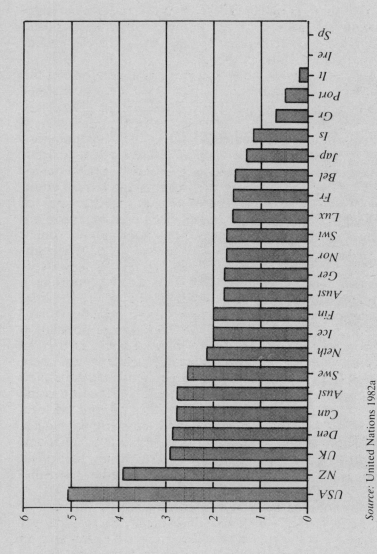

Source: United Nations 1982a

Figure 5.2 : Comparative divorce rates, 1981

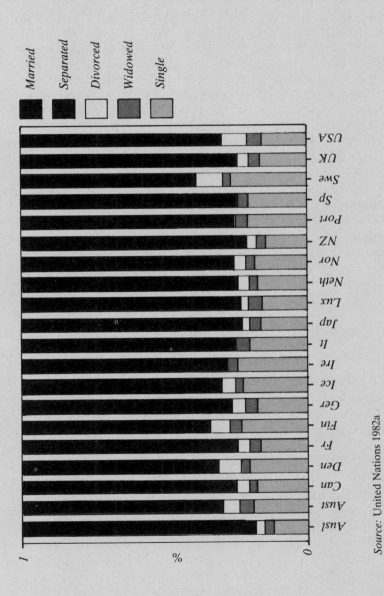

Legend: Married, Separated, Divorced, Widowed, Single

Countries: USA, UK, Swe, Sp, Port, NZ, Nor, Neth, Lux, Jap, It, Ire, Ice, Ger, Fin, Fr, Den, Can, Aust, Ausl

Source: United Nations 1982a

Figure 5.3 : Marital status of women, 1981 (Working age population)

tably led to an increase in the number of one-parent families, of which less than one in five are headed by men in European countries (EuroStat 1984: 57, 2). On this evidence the social lives of women have changed dramatically over the last decades. This can be interpreted as a positive development, depending upon one's view of the family and marriage, but this also represents a growth in the proportion of women who are vulnerable to poverty, especially single-parent mothers dependent upon low wages and welfare benefits. As Hilda Scott suggests, the same social trends may have a very different impact on both sexes. While divorce may liberate men from their family responsibilities, it is often the cause of female poverty (Scott 1984). Any analysis of the gains achieved by the women's movement over the last decades has to take account of these broad social trends. Within this context we need to see how far there have been changes in the selected indicators of educational opportunities, reproductive rights, maternity services and child-care facilities, all issues central to feminist demands.

EDUCATIONAL OPPORTUNITIES

Equal access to college education has long been recognised as a significant issue since formal qualifications are often the key to other social resources: élite status, career prospects, future economic rewards, technical knowledge and skills, as well as being valued in itself (Table 5.1). Over the last decades there has been a remarkable expansion of educational provisions, especially at the 'third level', which includes universities, polytechnics, colleges and technical institutes (UNESCO 1984). This growth has affected both sexes but it has been especially significant for women. Since the 1960s the average proportion of women in higher education increased from 30 to 43 per cent of all students in the countries under comparison. In many societies the growth over the last twenty years has been even more dramatic; women have moved from being a fifth to a half of all college students in Norway. Their numbers have

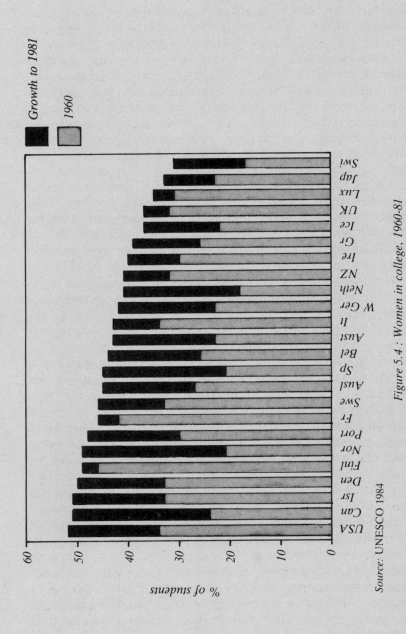

■ *Growth to 1981*

▨ *1960*

Figure 5.4 : Women in college, 1960-81

Source: UNESCO 1984

% *of students*

60 50 40 30 20 10 0

USA Can Isr Den Finl Nor Port Fr Swe Aust Sp Bel Aust It W Ger Neth NZ Ire Gr Ice UK Lux Jap Swi

doubled in Spain and the Netherlands, although in contrast women continue at only about a third of all students in Britain, Switzerland, Luxembourg and Japan (Fig. 5.4).

In many ways parallels can be drawn with women's increased participation in the labour force where, despite their increased numbers, women are still confined to certain sorts of work due to horizontal and vertical segregation. The same pattern exists in the sphere of higher education. With vertical segregation women are more strongly represented in undergraduate than postgraduate courses. Amongst doctoral students, for example, women are usually less than a quarter of all successful candidates even in countries where they are generally well represented at lower levels. Although the number of female university teachers has doubled over the last decade, they still constitute only a fifth of all staff, and there are even fewer in the higher-level positions within departments.

Despite women's increased access to educational institutions, there is continuing horizontal segregation by discipline. Educational segregation can be measured as the difference between the proportion of women studying a subject and the proportion of women in the total college population. This is consistent with the earlier definition of occupational segregation and it allows crosscultural comparisons separating segregation from other factors such as growth in the overall number of female students. As with earlier measures, if women constitute 35 per cent of all students, and 35 per cent of all those studying social science, then the coefficient will equal unity (1.00). If women are underrepresented in a discipline—for example, in the same population if only 9 per cent of engineers are women—then the coefficient will be less than unity (0.26).

On the basis of these measures women continue to study in traditionally female subjects in all the countries under comparison: dominating domestic science (1.68), teacher training (1.63), humanities (1.48) and fine art (1.38), while men predominate in such fields as engineering (0.16), architecture and town planning (0.63), mathematics and computer science (0.64) (UNESCO 1984). Women have been increasing in certain professional subjects, however, notably law (0.91) and medicine (1.28), which may lead to

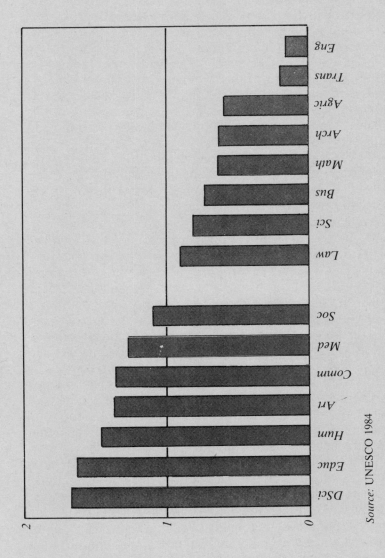

Source: UNESCO 1984

Figure 5.5: Educational segregation by subject, 1981 (1 = non-segregation)

significant future changes in the sex segregation of these occupations. Although these trends are apparent in all capitalist democracies, the extent of educational segregation varies widely between countries, with the most marked female underrepresentation in the Netherlands and Japan (Fig. 5.5). There is similar segregation by subject in vocational education and occupational training schemes (OECD 1985). Parallels can be drawn with the economic position of women; increasing numbers of women participate but horizontal and vertical segregation limits sexual equality.

Women now have increased access to higher education, but it has proved more difficult to transform the contents of the traditional curriculum and established methods of teaching and research with the development of a new feminist perspective (Spender 1981; Langland and Gove 1981; Culley and Portuges 1985). Since education may reinforce sexual stereotypes rather than challenge them, access by itself will not necessarily change the position of women. Some, like Rich, argue that women students are only tolerated in higher education so far as they fulfil masculine requirements—the cultivation of the competitive and hierarchical masculine skills that are taken as essential for conventional success:

As women have gradually and reluctantly been admitted into the mainstream of higher education they have been made participants in a system that prepares men to take up roles of power in a man-centered society, that asks questions and teaches 'facts' generated by a male intellectual tradition, and that subtly and openly confirms men as the leaders and shapers of human destiny. (Rich 1980: 127)

Attempts to change universities from within have met with some success; there has been a major expansion of women's studies over the last decades (European Commission 1984). This has resulted in the growth of a substantial body of feminist knowledge which aims to question the implicit bias in traditional research and transform the curricula (Spender 1981; Langland and Gove 1981). At the same time, feminists like Dale Spender are sceptical about the impact of women's studies on established disciplines, given the resistance of the educational system to

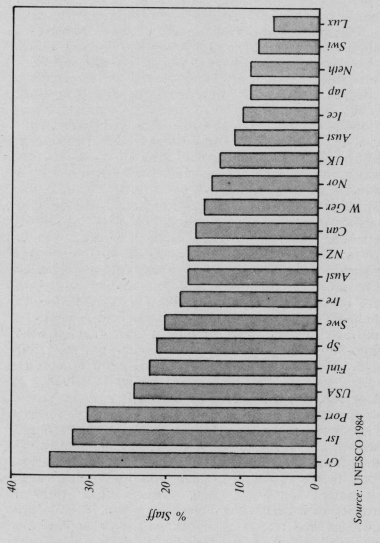

Figure 5.6 : Women college teachers, 1981

Source: UNESCO 1984

change (Spender 1985:188). The growth of women's studies cannot be directly documented in any quantifiable way, as the feminist perspective may be incorporated into mainstream courses and subsidiary options, as well as being taught in specific undergraduate and postgraduate courses. As an indirect indicator, however, we can compare the position of female teachers in colleges, to see where women are breaking through into positions of *potential* academic power where they are able to influence the curricula. As the results in Figure 5.6 show, although teaching is often seen as a 'natural' extension of women's work so that they predominate in nursery and junior schools, the same is not true at the higher level, where women hold about one in five university posts. There is considerable variation in this, however, with women particularly underrepresented in Switzerland, Japan and Britain.

On this basis we can conclude that the last decades have seen substantial improvements in the education of women. Their numbers in higher education have doubled in countries such as Norway, the Netherlands and Spain, and women now constitute more than half the college population in five out of the twenty-four countries under comparison. There remain substantial inequalities in a few societies, including Switzerland, Britain and Japan, but generally all countries display positive trends in educational participation. Subject segregation by sex remains but the trends are towards greater integration. Lastly, more women are breaking through into positions of academic influence as college teachers, although they remain a minority. There have also been improvements in the developing world over the last decades; the education gap between boys and girls at school is closing gradually and girls are edging forwards slightly faster in the race towards literacy (United Nations 1985a). In the liberal perspective, education is one of the most potent factors to change women's lives, through increasing their personal confidence, practical skills, critical knowledge and formal qualifications, which implies that these developments augur well for the future. This optimistic assessment, however, should be tempered by a note of caution. More women are gaining qualifications, but whether this will lead to better-paid employment opportuni-

Table 5.1: College education by subject, 1981

	Female over representation									Female under representation								
	Total	DSci	Educ	Hum	Art	Comm	Med	Soc	Av.	Law	Sci.	Bus.	Math.	Arch.	Agric.	Trans.	Eng.	Av.
Ausl	0.45	...	1.42	1.40	1.33	1.47	1.18	1.36	1.36	0.80	0.76	0.60	...	0.44	0.64	...	0.09	0.65
Aust	0.43	2.26	1.65	1.42	1.21	1.02	1.02	1.07	1.38	0.74	0.86	0.74	0.79	0.56	0.70	...	0.09	0.73
Bel	0.38	...	1.55	1.50	...	...	1.05	0.79	1.22	1.00	1.00	0.58	...	...	0.66	...	0.18	0.81
Can	0.51	1.88	1.37	1.02	1.24	1.16	1.41	1.16	1.32	0.78	0.67	0.94	0.71	0.41	0.63	0.12	0.18	0.61
Den	0.50	...	1.34	1.22	1.12	1.18	1.44	0.78	1.18	0.84	0.54	0.34	0.38	0.66	0.64	0.02	0.16	0.49
Finl	0.49	2.00	1.49	1.47	1.16	1.18	1.63	1.22	1.45	0.82	0.98	1.16	0.76	0.73	0.80	0.10	0.18	0.76
Ger	0.42	2.24	1.67	1.43	1.19	1.24	1.50	0.90	1.45	0.83	0.76	0.90	0.69	0.81	0.57	...	0.14	0.76
Ire	0.40	2.50	1.95	1.43	1.50	1.18	1.08	1.68	1.61	1.00	1.18	0.83	0.70	0.43	0.43	...	0.18	0.76
It(a)	0.44	...	1.66	1.80	1.27	...	0.84	1.07	1.33	1.00	1.32	0.75	0.95	0.75	0.52	...	0.11	0.88
Jap	0.33	0.30	2.15	2.00	2.15	...	1.12	0.33	1.34	...	0.42	...	0.61	...	0.39	...	0.06	0.47
Lux	0.35	...	1.71	1.66	...	...	1.40	1.69	1.61	1.71	0.83	...	...	...	...	...	0.09	1.27
Neth	0.41	1.78	1.46	1.20	1.15	1.61	1.22	2.02	1.35	0.83	0.46	0.44	0.34	...	0.56	0.05	0.22	0.45
Nor	0.49	2.00	1.45	1.14	1.16	1.51	1.49	1.00	1.39	0.80	0.57	0.69	0.59	0.78	0.61	0.29	0.31	0.62
NZ	0.42	0.23	1.83	1.50	1.52	1.40	1.40	1.45	1.34	0.98	0.81	0.79	0.62	0.57	0.57	0.17	0.07	0.64
Port	0.48	1.17	1.63	1.50	1.25	1.54	1.25	0.96	1.33	0.73	1.17	0.67	0.48	0.69	0.77	...	0.35	0.75
Sp	0.45	...	1.53	1.47	1.13	1.00	1.20	1.02	1.23	0.84	1.02	0.82	0.84	0.38	0.71	...	0.18	0.77
Swe	0.46	2.04	1.65	1.37	1.33	1.37	1.50	1.13	1.48	0.93	0.74	0.89	0.50	0.87	0.72	0.22	0.26	0.70
Swi	0.31	1.10	1.97	1.65	2.16	1.55	1.16	1.16	1.53	0.90	0.68	0.55	0.55	0.81	0.03	0.74	0.10	0.61
UK	0.37	2.32	1.65	1.65	1.51	2.03	1.38	1.22	1.68	1.08	0.89	0.84	0.70	0.76	0.86	0.11	0.11	0.75
USA(b)	0.50	...	1.54	...	...	...	1.30	1.02	1.29	0.60	0.68	0.78	0.74	0.52	0.58	0.24	0.22	0.59
Av.	0.43	1.68	1.63	1.46	1.38	...	1.28	1.10	1.39	0.91	0.82	0.74	0.64	0.63	0.60	0.20	0.16	0.70

Note: (a) 1982 (b) 1978: third-level education. The ratio is calculated as % of women in subject over % of women in college.
Educ = Education and teacher training; Hum. = Humanities; Soc. = Social science; Bus = Business administration; Comm. = Mass communications; DSci = Domestic science; Sci. = Natural science; Math. = Mathematics and computer science; Med. = Medical and health science; Eng. = Engineering; Arch. = Architecture and planning; Trans. = Transport; Agric. = Agriculture
Source: UNESCO 1984; *Digest of Educational Statistics 1981* (USA)

ties is open to question. Research in general indicates that differences in education between women and men does little to explain the earnings gap (OECD 1985). In the United States, for example, there is evidence that at every level of qualifications women continue to earn less than men. Female graduates with fifteen years of education earn on average less than men who have completed only twelve years of schooling (United States, 1983). College education is also primarily available to certain social groups, particularly those who are middle class, affluent and white; opportunities are not necessarily available for all groups of women. Therefore, how far increased educational opportunities change the status of women depends on other structural factors in society.

REPRODUCTIVE RIGHTS

While expanding educational opportunities for women has been a relatively non-controversial issue, the same cannot be said for the question of reproductive rights, which has proved a highly emotive issue, polarising public opinion into opposing camps. To understand the difference, we can use the distinction made by Butler and Stokes between vallance and positional issues (Butler and Stokes 1974). Vallance issues are those where the public is largely in agreement about goals, such as the need to reduce unemployment and inflation, and discussion is limited to the question of means. In contrast with positional issues, such as the redistribution of wealth, public opinion is deeply divided about the actual goals to be pursued. Gelb and Palley suggest that the women's movement has been more successful with vallance issues, such as equality of educational opportunity, than more controversial positional issues like reproductive rights (Gelb and Palley 1983; Outshoorn 1986). In so far as public opinion on abortion is polarised, and the issue is highly salient, politicians will significantly alienate one group of voters, whatever their position. The abortion campaign has mobilised a large number of supporters in public demonstrations, but in reaction a well-organised opposition has developed. Due to this, parties may well be reluctant to take a clear stand on reproductive rights, preferring a bipartisan approach in which the issue is left to be decided by the individual representative.

Within this context, how far does legal access to abortion vary cross-culturally? The last decades have seen a remarkable trend towards more liberal abortion laws in almost all developed societies, while only a few countries have moved in a more restrictive direction (Francome 1984). The most liberal grounds are abortion on the *request* of the woman concerned, which in 1985 was legally available in about a third of the countries under comparison (Table 5.2). Other societies recognise abortion for *socio-economic* reasons, such as the effect of childbirth upon the health and welfare of the woman's existing family. More restrictive grounds include the *foetal* criteria concerning likely physical or mental abnormality of the child if born, the *juridical* criteria if pregnancy was the result of rape or incest, the *therapeutic* criteria of risk to the woman's physical or mental health, and the most limited criteria of threat to the *woman's life* (Cook and Dickens 1979). The conditions legalising abortion also vary cross-culturally in terms of the length of pregnancy during which abortion is authorised, conditions of funding, the bureaucratic and medical procedures to qualify and the practical availability of services. On the basis of these differences we can develop a typology, following the method of Field (1979), to rank countries from most to least liberal.

There is a broad pattern with the earliest legalisation on abortion in the Nordic countries, Switzerland and Japan. Abortion was authorised in Iceland, Sweden and Denmark on social/medical and eugenic grounds in the inter-war period, followed by Finland in 1951 and Norway in 1965. There was a further liberalisation to permit abortion on request in Denmark (1970–3), Sweden (1975) and Norway (1978) (Francome 1984). In Japan abortion has a long tradition, having been legal since 1948 for foetal, judicial, medical and social-economic reasons, although there have been a number of attempts to restrict the grounds in the early 1970s (Morgan 1984). With Commonwealth countries sharing a common legal heritage, including Canada, New

Table 5.2: Legal grounds for granting abortion, 1984

	Life of mother	Health of mother	Juridical	Foetal	Socio-economic	On request
Ausl	xxxxxxxxxxxxxxxxx					
Aust	xxxxxxxxxxxxxxxxxxxxxxxxxxxxxxxxxxxxxxxxxxxxxxxxxxxxxxxx					
Bel	xxxxxxxxxxxxxxxxx					
Can	xxxxxxxxxxxxxxxxx					
Den	xxxxxxxxxxxxxxxxxxxxxxxxxxxxxxxxxxxxxxxxxxxxxxxxxxxxxxxx					
Fr	xxxxxxxxxxxxxxxxxxxxxxxxxxxxxxxxxxxxxxxxxxxxxxxxxxxxxxxx					
Fin	xxxxxxxxxxxxxxxxxxxxxxxxxxxxxxxxxxxxxxxxxxxxxxxxxx					
Ger	xxxxxxxxxxxxxxxxxxxxxxxxxxxxxxxxxxxxxxxxxxxxxxxxxx					
Gr	xxxxxxxxxxx					
Ice	xxxxxxxxxxxxxxxxxxxxxxxxxxxxxxxxxxxxxxxxxxxxxxx					
Ire	xxxxxxxxx					
Isr	xxxxxxxxxxxxxxxxxxxxxxxxxxxxxxxxxxxxxxxxxxxxxxx					
It	xxxxxxxxxxxxxxxxxxxxxxxxxxxxxxxxxxxxxxxxxxxxxxxxxxxxxxxx					
Jap	xxxxxxxxxxxxxxxxxxxxxxxxxxxxxxxxxxxxxxxxxxxxxxx					
Lux	xxxxxxxxxxxxxxxxxxxxxxxxxxxxxxxxxxxxxxxxxxxxxxx					
Neth	xxxxxxxxxxxxxxxxxxxxxxxxxxxxxxxxxxxxxxxxxxxxxxxxxxxxxxxx					
Nor	xxxxxxxxxxxxxxxxxxxxxxxxxxxxxxxxxxxxxxxxxxxxxxxxxxxxxxxx					
NZ	xxxxxxxxxxxxxxxxxxxxxxxxxxxxxxxxxxxx					
Port	xxxxxxxxxxxxxxxxxxxxxxxxxxxxxxxxxxx					
Sp	xxxxxxxxx					
Swe	xxxxxxxxxxxxxxxxxxxxxxxxxxxxxxxxxxxxxxxxxxxxxxxxxxxxxxxx					
UK	xxxxxxxxxxxxxxxxxxxxxxxxxxxxxxxxxxxxxxxxxxxxxxxxxx					
USA	xxxxxxxxxxxxxxxxxxxxxxxxxxxxxxxxxxxxxxxxxxxxxxxxxxxxxxxx					
World-wide % of countries*	99%	51%	28%	28%	17%	12%

Note: * Since countries allow more than one reason for abortion this does not total 100 per cent. N. 144 countries provided information in the United Nations survey.
Sources: United Nations (1982b), Francome (1984), Cook and Dickens (1979).

Zealand and Australia, abortion has been liberalised following the British 1967 Act, although abortion on request has still not been accepted (Cook and Dickens 1979). In the United States abortion has been legally available on request since the *Roe v. Wade* Supreme Court decision in 1973, although again there have been several well-organised attempts to restrict access, and public funding has been withdrawn. In Western Europe most countries introduced abortion reforms in the 1970s, with the most liberal grounds in Austria (1975), Italy (1978), France (1975) and the

Netherlands (1981). In other Catholic countries the situation is more varied. In Portugal, for instance, abortion was legalised on the grounds of the woman's health, foetal and juridical criteria in 1984, although the following year in Spain a similar law was rejected on constitutional grounds. In Ireland not only is abortion illegal but any attempts at reform have been made more difficult by the 1983 constitutional amendment to guarantee the 'equal rights to life of the unborn' (Morgan 1984). Therefore, overall during the 1970s there has been a world-wide move to relax abortion laws. As a result, within capitalist democracies women have access to abortion on demand in about a third of all countries, and only in a few societies are reproductive rights severely restricted.

Since there is often a difference between *de jure* and *de facto* women's rights we need to go further to compare the implementation of abortion policies. The practical conditions for abortion vary widely due to the provision of services in hospitals and clinics, the bureaucratic qualifying procedures, the costs of the service and the availability of information and advice. Practical constraints, such as the non-cooperation of medical personnel and hospital administrators, may limit the intentions of a law in the implementation stage. Although abortion is legalised, women may still find it easier to travel abroad for the operation. To compare reproductive rights, therefore, we need to analyse the outcome as well as the type of abortion policies. To assess these services we can compare the legal abortion rates per 1,000 women of reproductive age. In practice abortion may be more widely available, through women travelling abroad for abortions or obtaining them illegally, but the legal rate is a good indicator of the provision of official medical services. As Figure 5.7 shows, legal abortion rates vary widely, with the rate highest in the United States, where one in three pregnancies ends in abortion. As we might expect, there is an association between the type of abortion law and the rate of abortion ($r = .59$) in the eighteen countries for which data are available.

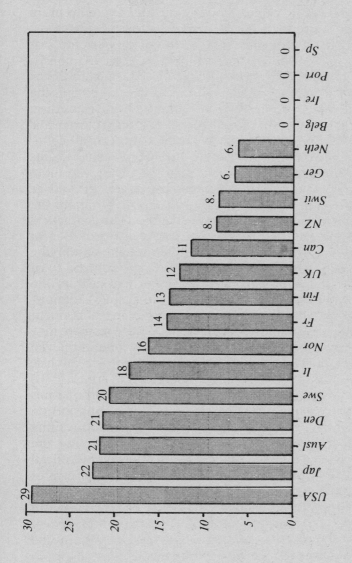

Figure 5.7 : Legal abortion rates, 1980: rates /1000 women (15-44)

Source: Francome 1984

FAMILY PLANNING

Abortion, however, cannot be seen in isolation from other questions of reproductive control. The women's movement has also demanded an increase in the availability of safe contraceptives, including state funding of services, family-planning advice centres and information campaigns. Given the attendant health problems associated with the pill and some innovative contraceptives, there has also been pressure for increased medical research into this area and improved screening for cervical cancer.

The legal provision of access to contraceptives has evolved in a liberal direction in the last decades. In a United Nations survey amongst thirty-nine developed countries, thirty-three had access to contraception authorised and supported by the governments directly or indirectly (United Nations 1984b). Since 1978 Greece, Ireland and Spain have taken legal steps to authorise access to contraceptives, although in Ireland it has been suggested in a recent survey that, even with these developments, from a half to three-quarters of pharmacists were refusing to stock contraceptives (Morgan 1984). There is also cross-cultural variation in how far birth-control services are subsidised or provided free, restricted to married couples or those over a minimum age, and requiring a prescription or available over the counter in chemists shops.

Due to this liberalisation, the general trend in Western countries during the 1970s has been one of increasing use of contraceptives, but the level may have reached a ceiling. In those developed countries for which information is available it has been estimated that two-thirds of married couples were using contraceptives, especially the pill and sterilisation. Most of those not using contraception believed themselves to be infecund, currently pregnant or they wished to be pregnant. Less than 10 per cent of married women were not using contraceptives and were therefore exposed to the risk of unwanted pregnancy (United Nations 1984a). As Figure 5.8 shows, available data suggests that there is considerable cross-cultural variation in the use of contraceptives, although national surveys are not necessarily reliable

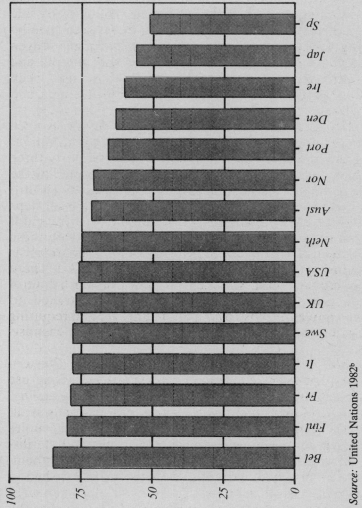

Source: United Nations 1982[b]

Figure 5.8 : Comparative use of contraceptives, 1981:
% married women (15-44)

in this field. Medical records are usually thorough, but this does not include information on contraceptives available without prescription. The data suggests, however, that as might be expected contraceptive use is more limited in traditional Catholic countries including Ireland, Portugal and Spain, although use is also relatively low in Japan and Denmark. Unlike findings in some other studies, within the countries under comparison there seems to be no significant relationship between the rates of abortion and contraception ($r = .19$).

CHILD-CARE AND MATERNITY SERVICES

Given the traditional role of women within the family, another primary goal of the women's movement has been to extend the provision of nursery schools, crèches, day-care and kindergarten places. The aim has been to enable women to have state-funded child-care available as a right, especially for women in employment. Publicly provided child-care services are measured for comparative purposes as the proportion of places in education preceding the first level of compulsory schooling (UNESCO 1984). It would have been useful to compare government spending on pre-primary kindergartens and nursery schools, but this data is not disaggregated from general educational expenditure for all countries. Many other informal child-care arrangements may be available, with private child-minders within the locality, members of the extended family or neighbourhood co-operatives, but these are not included in the analysis since they are not the direct result of public policies. The general trends in capitalist democracies over the last decades show a striking growth in the provision of child-care services, especially in Scandinavia, Britain and Portugal, although by 1981 on average there are only places for about a quarter of all children under school age (Fig. 5.9). It remains questionable, therefore, whether this meets the increased demand, given the rise in the proportion of working mothers and single-parent families since the 1960s.

Lastly, we can use the maternal mortality rate as one of

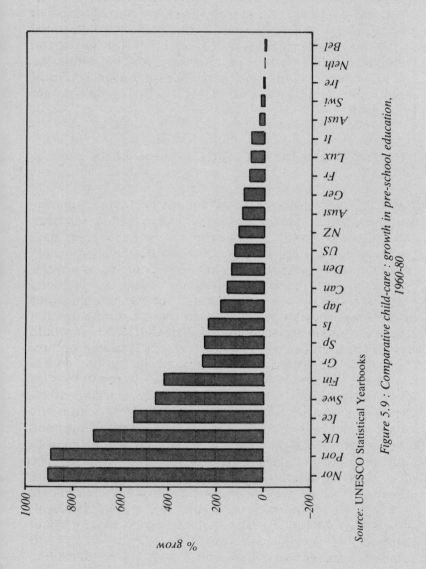

Figure 5.9 : Comparative child-care : growth in pre-school education, 1960–80

Source: UNESCO Statistical Yearbooks

the most commonly used social indicators to compare the standard of health care for prenatal and childbirth services. From 1970 to 1980 maternal mortality declined in almost all countries under comparison, with the rate dramatically reduced by a half in West Germany, Italy and Japan (Fig. 5.10), and exceptionally low in Sweden and the Netherlands (United Nations 1985). As the United Nations concluded in their world-wide survey, the new emphasis on primary health-care for pregnant women, including prenatal check-ups, immunisation and advice on child-care, nutrition and breast-feeding, have reduced maternal and infant mortality rates in many countries. Many of the dangers faced by women in childbirth can now be avoided if women are examined early in their pregnancy to check for abnormalities, given the advances in gynaecological knowledge (United Nations 1985a). In the countries under comparison, in the last decade alone the average rate of maternal mortality has dropped from twenty-nine per 100,000 births to fourteen per 100,000, although there are still considerable cross-national variations in these rates.

EXPLANATIONS OF SOCIAL EQUALITY

On this basis we need to move from the description of cross-cultural differences in the social lives of women towards a comparative explanation. In particular, we need to examine whether political or environmental factors have had most impact on these social indicators. The explanatory model that we will investigate is illustrated in Figure 5.11. On the one hand, *environmental* variables might be expected to play a major role in determining the level and provision of services relating to education, contraception, child-care, prenatal health-care and abortion. As discussed in the first chapter, a number of studies have argued that economic growth and the level of economic development are the factors most strongly associated with the provision of government services (Dye 1969; Cutright 1965; Parkin 1971; Wilensky 1975; Jackman 1980). In this view there are general pressures in all industrialised countries for a set of

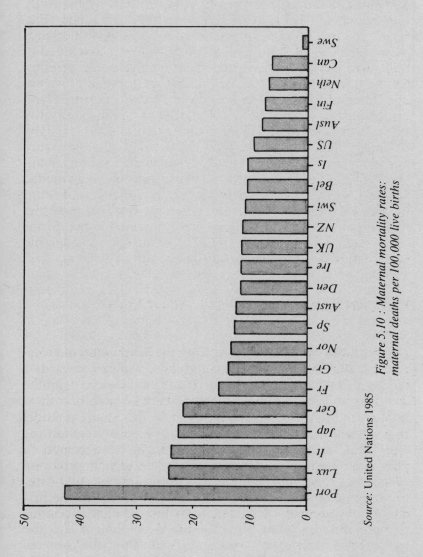

*Figure 5.10 : Maternal mortality rates:
maternal deaths per 100,000 live births*

Source: United Nations 1985

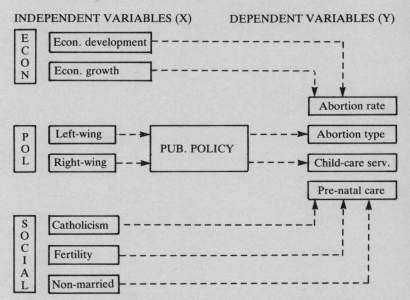

INDEPENDENT VARIABLES (X)   DEPENDENT VARIABLES (Y)

Figure 5.11 : Casual model of reproductive and child-care policies

welfare programmes to cover the health, education and well-being of its citizens. In the functional view, similar demographic and economic secular trends have affected capitalist democracies, to which governments have responded irrespective of their party-political persuasion. It can be argued that the substantial increase in educational opportunities for all sectors of the population in most societies is due to the need for a well-trained and educated labour force to cope with the increased demands of complex technology, the expansion of the service sector and the decline of manufacturing. Recognising this need, governments have sought to increase the provision of educational opportunities to create the conditions for economic growth, irrespective of their commitment to using education as an agency of social mobility. In the functionalist view, the logic of modern industrialism and economic development leads to a convergence of societies, with the development of a similar range of public policies (Kerr 1960). Some argue further that given the development of 'catch-all' parties, who try to win votes from all social groups, the partisan composition of government will have little affect on vallance issues (Bell 1960). If there is a broad consensus of public

opinion favouring the expansion of educational opportunities, and parties are non-ideological, then both Conservatives and Social Democrats will pursue similar policies to
maximise their attraction to the electorate.

Similar arguments can be advanced for the provision of
reproductive and child-care services, although the issues are
different in significant ways. In the functionalist perspective
trends in the traditional pattern of the family, marriage and
divorce have affected all societies in recent years, forcing
both left- and right-wing governments to respond to the
policy problems which this has caused. During the 1970s
there was a remarkably uniform trend in Western societies
to liberalise abortion and divorce laws, and improve
maternity, family planning and child-care services. Medical
and technological trends, such as improvements in contraception and gynaecological research, have had a world-wide
impact, allowing more women to control their fertility and
improving the standards of maternity care. Reproductive
rights raise different types of issues to the question of
educational opportunities. In so far as these can be seen as
'moral'- rather than 'class'-based issues then we might
expect that left–right party divisions had less importance
than religious differences between parties (Outshoorn
1986). Some suggest that cultural factors such as the strength
of Catholicism are better predictors of a country's policies
on abortion than the strength of Socialist or Conservative
parties (Field 1979). In addition, parties may be reluctant
to take a clear-cut stance on position issues like abortion or
contraception, since they may alienate significant groups of
voters (Outshoorn 1986).

Others argue in contrast that *party political* factors can
have a significant impact on the social position of women.
The 'end of ideology' thesis has received strong criticism
for the argument that all parties follow middle-of-the-road
consensus policies. Others suggest that political ideology
continues to divide parties in terms of their rhetoric and
policy goals. Socialist and Conservative governments will
be constrained by similar circumstances, but they will not
respond to such problems as unemployment or inflation in
the same way. If ideology does play a role in policy forma-
tion, in so far as Socialist parties have a more egalitarian

and interventionist commitment, we might expect left-wing
governments to take a more active role in expanding services
which affect women and the family. Governments have a
range of policy instruments to increase educational opportunities for women and social minorities, including legislation on sex discrimination, affirmative-action
programmes, positive occupational training programmes,
initiatives to change sex biases in the curriculum and in
teaching practices, and active recruitment and counselling
services. Several countries have also established special
commissions with responsibility for reducing sex inequalities
in education. It may be difficult for policy initiatives to have
a significant impact on sexual inequalities in so far as they
are the result of informal practices, traditional attitudes and
the 'hidden curricula' rather than formal discrimination.
However, through positive quota systems, such as those
used in Swedish vocational training schemes and affirmative-
action programmes in the United States, governments can
directly intervene to change sex segregation in education.

Again, with the issues of abortion, family planning,
maternity and child-care it might be expected that left-wing
governments would expand services as part of their commitment to the welfare state. Further, it has been suggested
that right-wing politicians in virtually all societies have taken
a more restrictive position on abortion than left-wing ones
(Francome 1984: 210). Francome suggests this is due to
Conservative politicians believing that the social order
depends on restrictions on sexuality. The longer abortion
rights exist, the less threatening they will seem to the social
order, and therefore the less right-wing politicians will
oppose this issue. To compare the impact of political parties
on the indicators of reproductive rights and welfare services,
we can use covariance structure analysis (Lisrel).

CONCLUSIONS

The results of this analysis suggest that political parties have
their greatest impact on positional rather than vallance
issues. Where there is a high degree of consensus in public

opinion about the appropriate goals for government to follow, on such matters as maternity health-care and educational opportunities, then partisan differences tend not to influence policy output. In contrast, where public controversy exists about both policy ends and means, on such positional issues as reproductive rights, then political factors tend to have a significant impact.

As the results show in the causal model in Figure 5.12, right-wing parties were found to have a major influence on restricting legal abortion rights whilst left-wing parties were associated with more liberal legislation. More unexpectedly, in recent years Catholicism was found to have no restrictive effect on abortion laws. This can be explained by comparing the legal status of abortion given in Table 5.2. By the mid-1980s, with the notable exceptions of Ireland and Spain, many of the countries where Catholicism is strongest have established some of the most liberal legal grounds for abortion, such as Italy, Austria and France. In contrast, predominantly Protestant countries, such as Canada, Australia and New Zealand, followed the more restricted British model, which does not recognise abortion on request. As a result, although religion may have influenced the pace of abortion reform, by the mid-1980s many Catholic countries had more liberal abortion laws than many Protestant societies.

At the policy implementation stage, however, environmental factors did play a significant role. Although formal legal rights to abortion may be established, in practice abortion may be limited by the provision of services in hospitals and clinics, the availability of advice and information, the non-cooperation of medical professionals and general social attitudes. The results of the analysis suggest that parties shape the legal framework, which indirectly affects the abortion rate, but abortion services in a country tend to be more directly influenced by religious and economic factors. The influence of Catholicism means that such countries as Italy have established liberal *de jure* abortion rights, but in practice the use of these services is restricted by social attitudes and mores.

In terms of welfare rights it is apparent that right-wing parties tend to restrict the provision of child-care facilities,

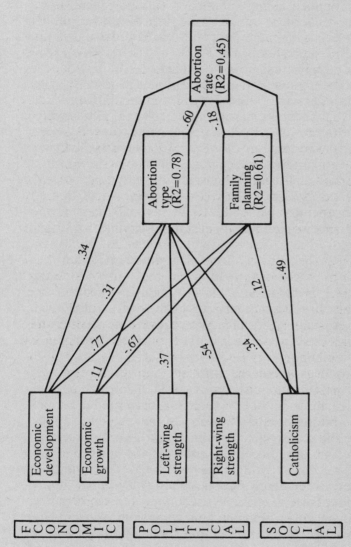

Figure 5.12: Causal model of reproductive rights

Note: See Figure 4.7 for sources. Estimates are based on Lisrel Maximum Likelihood Coefficients. Only statistically significant relationships are reported (p. = >0.05). The overall model has a goodness of fit of 0.977 (adjusted, 0.86) and the Total Coefficient of Determination for structural equations is 0.92.

although political factors have no significant impact on maternity services. Overall the model fails to explain cross-cultural variations in the proportion of women in college, since this seems to be the result of specific factors outside of the explanatory framework, such as educational opportunities in earlier schooling.

On this basis we can conclude that over the last decades there have been radical developments in reproductive rights and welfare services, generally in a liberal direction, although the pace of change varies substantially between societies. By the mid-1980s women had achieved greater sexual autonomy through a general expansion of family-planning services and the legalisation of abortion in nearly all Western democracies. There had been other positive developments: maternity services had improved the safety of childbirth, public child-care services had rapidly expanded and women made substantial advances in higher education.

Evaluating the impact of Socialist governments on these changes in the social position of women is a complex matter. On the basis of this analysis it can be concluded that political parties have had their greatest impact on *positional* issues, including abortion rights and child-care facilities, rather than vallance issues such as educational opportunities, maternity and family-planning services. With the latter there is a broad social consensus about the need to improve the safety of prenatal, post-natal and contraceptive health-care, while medical advances in gynaecological research have reduced maternal and infant mortality in most developed countries. There are still many political controversies about the ethical, financial and practical consequences of implementing prenatal and family-planning services, including the provision of screening for cervical cancer, research into the safety of contraceptive methods, new advances in medical techniques in embryology, and the confidentiality of services for the young. In most Western countries, however, the provision of family-planning facilities has become accepted as a necessary part of the health service. As vallance issues, there is high degree of public agreement about policy ends, and controversy centres largely about questions of means. The same case can be made for the question of equal access

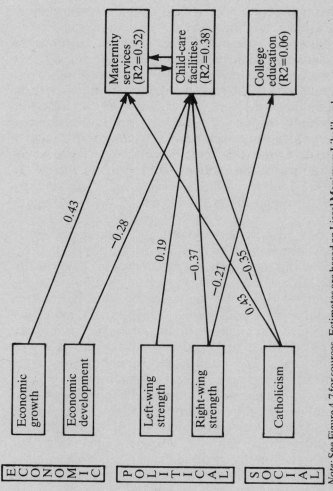

Figure 5.13 : Casual model of welfare rights

Note: See Figure 4.7 for sources. Estimates are based on Lisrel Maximum Likelihood Coefficients. Only statistically significant relationships are reported (p. = 0.01). The overall model has a goodness of fit of 0.99 (adjusted, 0.93) and the Total Coefficient of Determination for Structural Equations is 0.70.

to education; disagreement continues about such questions as positive discrimination, but the need to increase educational opportunities for women and minorities is broadly accepted. With vallance issues, parties tend to follow indistinguishable policies, to maximise their support in terms of public opinion. In contrast, party politics has a stronger impact on *positional* issues, such as abortion and child-care services, where there are considerable division within public opinion about the appropriate policy goals to be pursued. The results suggest that, within the overall socio-economic context, on these issues party politics does matter, especially the role of right-wing parties in restricting change. It remains to be seen whether these partisan differences continue in the sphere of political élites, where the thesis that parties matter can be tested most rigorously.

6 The Political Position of Women in Élites

As we have seen, sexual stratification exists in the distribution of material rewards and social prestige, but inequalities are most marked in the dimension of political power. There is a general tendency for men to dominate positions of public power in all societies: past and present, developed and underdeveloped, capitalist or communist, urban or rural. Not that women are without influence, especially through their role in the household, their kinship ties or through mutual solidarity, but according to most anthropological evidence, matriarchy seems to have been a myth. Everywhere women are substantially underrepresented in political élites whether within parties, legislatures, cabinets, governments, bureaucracies, the judiciary, public bodies or the corporate sphere of trade-union and business interest groups. Recently however, women have been making significant breakthroughs into political élites in certain societies such as the Netherlands, Norway, Finland and Denmark, so we need to analyse how far traditional patterns are changing.

To analyse sexual inequalities in public power we will again see whether this has been the result of political or environmental variables. On the *political* side, if the Left are committed to sexual equality, in practice as well as in rhetoric, then we would expect to find more women within Socialist parties in prominent positions as parliamentary representatives and party leaders. The connection between parties and sexual equality is relatively direct; they do not need measures of public policy to reduce sexual discrimination as potentially parties have considerable power to promote women to positions of influence within their own ranks. Others suggest that amongst political variables the electoral system can play a major role in facilitating women's entry into the political system, especially if the system is proportional rather than majoritarian. Alternatively, some suggest that *environmental* factors might have more influence on the position of women in élites, including whether the socio-economic position of women qualifies them for office and whether cultural attitudes are favourable towards women in politics.

Studies of women in political élites are severly hampered by the lack of reliable comparative data. Not only is it difficult to compare representatives in diverse political institutions—such as county councillors in Britain, legislators in cantonal parliaments in Switzerland, state senators in the United States and members of the French regional assemblies—but often we lack basic information about the number of women who stood or were elected to office. We often know even less about the proportion of women in other areas of public life, as executive officers in major governmental agencies, committee members on public bodies, active participants in major political parties or leaders of trade unions. This information is rarely published in statistical yearbooks or official records and no international agency gathers this data in standardised format, although recently the United Nations and the Council of Europe have made some moves in this direction (United Nations 1985b; Mossuz-Lavau and Sineau 1984). For these reasons we need to be cautious in drawing conclusions about women in public office based on statistical sources. To overcome these problems we will limit the main analysis to the position of women within national legislatures and major political parties in Western democracies, since this gives a reasonably reliable basis for comparison.

WOMEN IN LEGISLATIVE OFFICE

If we turn first to the position of women in national legislatures, it is clear that in recent years there are striking contrasts between countries. Nowhere do women achieve equal representation, but there are a relatively high number of women (15 to 31 per cent) in Sweden, Finland, Denmark, Norway and the Netherlands (Fig. 6.1). At a slightly lower level, about 10 per cent of parliamentary representatives were female in Portugal, West Germany and Switzerland, while there are very few (<5 per cent) in such countries as Japan, Britain, Canada, Greece, America, Australia and Spain. As these contrasts between countries continue at other levels of government, this suggests that they reflect systematic social differences. Where women get on in national office they are likely to do well in local government; there is a strong association between the two (r = .90), although there are some exceptions to this pattern.

At the international level an analysis of the results of the 1984 direct elections to the European Parliament has the advantage of allowing the comparison of candidates from a range of liberal democracies in a simultaneous election for the same office. National differences in the campaigns remain; in particular, the electoral system was not the same throughout the Community. However, the results allow more uniform comparisons for European countries than other data. As the results in the Table 6.1 show, cross-cultural differences in the representation of women in local and national political élites parallel those found in the European Parliament. Where women politicians are strongly represented nationally, such as in Denmark and the Netherlands, they have also usually done well in the European Parliament, and the reverse is true of countries like the United Kingdom and Italy. In general, women are more strongly represented at the European level. In the 1984 elections there were seventy-five women elected out of 434 representatives, or 17 per cent of the total, which is double the proportion in equivalent national parliaments. This also represents a considerable change since the first Common Assembly of the EC (1952–8) when only one woman was nominated out of the seventy-eight members (1.3 per cent). This increased marginally to 3 per cent of the members by 1972 and 5.5 per cent by 1978, but it was only with the direct elections of 1979 that there was a real breakthrough to 16 per cent of MEPs.[1] The proportion of women in

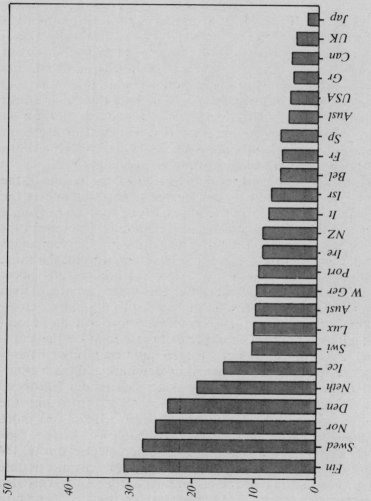

Figure 6.1 : Women in national legislatures, 1983

Table 6.1: Proportion of women in legislatures (%)

Country	Date	National			Local		European	Source:
		Lower Hs	Upper Hs	Cabinet	Regional	City	1984	
Finland	1983	31	n.r.	18	..	22	n.r.	Skaard 1983
Sweden	1983	28	n.r.	26	31	29	n.r.	Skaard 1983
Norway	1983	26	n.r.	22	29	23	n.r.	Skaard 1983
Denmark	1983	24	n.r	15	20	21	38	Skaard 1983
Netherlands	1984	19	19	12	16.5	13	28	Embassy
Iceland	1983	15	n.r.	10	..	12	n.r.	Skaard 1983
Switzerland	1979	11	7	..	..	..	n.r	European Commission
Luxembourg	1982	10	..	..	..	..	17	European Commission 1983
Austria	1981	10	..	..	..	..	n.r	
W. Germany	1983	10	5	..	8	11	20	European Commission 1983
Portugal	1982	10	..	..	..	..	n.r.	
Ireland	1983	9	10	..	5	..	13	Smyth 1984
New Zealand	1982	9	n.r.	10	7	20	n.4.	
Italy	1983	8	4	..	4	3	10	
Israel	1983	8	3	..	..	..	n.r	Embassy
Belgium	1983	6	12	..	..	..	17	European Commission 1983
France	1982	6	3	11	14	3	21	Embassy
Spain	1980	5	14	..	..	..	n.r	Matsell
Australia	1983	5	19	..	7	6	n.r	Simms 1984; Walmsley 1982
USA	1984	5	2	16	13	10	n.r	CAMP 1984
Greece	1983	4	..	..	..	..	n.r	
Canada	1984	4	(N. 9)	7	8	..	n.r	Embassy
UK	1983	4	7	1	16	18	15	Bristow 1980; *Times* 1979
Japan	1982	2	7	..	1	2	n.r	Embassy
Average		13	8	15	15	15	20	

the European Parliament is even more remarkable when compared with other international organisations such as the Council of Europe and the United Nations, where women constitute less than 10 per cent of delegates (Thom 1981).

At the level of cabinet members and heads of government, there have been so few that we cannot generalise with any reliability. Those which have been elected to prime ministerial and presidential office in capitalist democracies include Britain's Margaret Thatcher, Israel's Golda Meir, Iceland's Vigdes Finnbogadottir and Norway's Gro Brundtland. With the possible exception of the latter two countries, it cannot be said that women as a group have made important breakthroughs to power in these nations. Instead, particular individuals have used a combination of luck, ability and talent to take advantage of particular circumstances which led to their rise to power (Boutilier 1978; Vallance 1979).

There have been few women in cabinet office in any of the countries under comparison, although again there is a consistent pattern since the countries with the most women in their elected assemblies also have the most women in government. Women have tended to be more strongly represented in the Scandinavian countries; Finnish governments usually include two or three women, and in the 1980 Swedish government five out of twenty cabinet ministers were women (Skaard 1983; Haavio-Mannila). Amongst Western countries, Britain is fairly typical with no cabinets including more than two female ministers, while there have been no women in recent cabinets in Switzerland, Italy and the United States. In addition, women who are included within government are usually restricted to certain areas of ministerial responsibility, especially departments of education, consumer affairs, welfare and health. A few countries, including France and Canada, have introduced ministries to deal exclusively with the status of women, although this is usually handled by other departments such as the Ministry of Labour (Italy, Luxembourg and Sweden), Consumer Affairs (Norway), Youth, Family Affairs and Health (West Germany), the Prime Minister's Office (Belgium, Denmark, Finland, Greece, Italy, Japan and Portugal) or independent commissions (Britain, United

States, the Netherlands, Spain, Iceland) (United Nations 1985; Mossuz-Lavau and Sineau 1984).

If we turn to general trends over time, it is apparent that the differences between countries have been growing since the 1960s (Fig. 6.2). The number of women in national office in Britain, United States and Japan has remained steady or even declined over the years, despite the impression commonly given in the media of gradual progress. On the other hand, since the war there has been continuous growth in the proportion of female legislators in Scandinavia, and the percentage has quadrupled in the Netherlands. There is distinct evidence of recent improvements in France, Ireland and Italy, although the extent of the change should not be exaggerated. Even Switzerland and Australia, which in the early 1970s had no women in their parliaments, have changed. Yet trends are static in the US Congress or the British Parliament despite pressure from an activist women's movement and the individual success of exceptional leaders such as Mrs Margaret Thatcher and Congresswoman Geraldine Ferraro. Despite these well-known leaders in 1983, there were only twenty-four women out of 535 members of the US Congress and twenty-three women out of 650 MPs in Britain. There are no longer any legal obstacles to the election of women to political office in any of the countries under comparison, with the exception of certain cantons in Switzerland, where women still cannot vote or stand in local elections. So how do we explain why women politicians are getting on further and faster in some political systems rather than others?

POLITICAL AND ENVIRONMENTAL EXPLANATIONS

In the *environmental* sphere, explanations tend to emphasise either *cultural attitudes* or the *socio-economic background* of women. Those who emphasise the role of culture suggest that in Western democracies women have been elected in the greatest numbers in countries with a Nordic heritage, while women have done least well in societies characterised

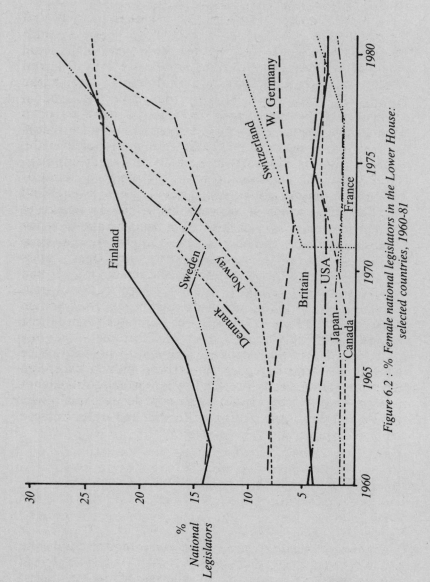

Figure 6.2 : % Female national legislators in the Lower House: selected countries, 1960-81

by a common Anglo-American culture (Britain, America, Australia, Canada, New Zealand) and many of the countries of Southern Europe (including Spain and Greece). Is it the case, therefore, that Scandinavians share liberal attitudes towards the role of women while other societies have more conservative and traditional values?

Cultural attitudes may play an important role in the three hurdles candidates have to cross to achieve office, since women must be willing to stand, they must be judged suitable candidates by the party selectorate and they must be given support by the voters. If attitudes towards female candidates are negative, this could be expected to influence the number of women who want to run for office, who feel that it would be an appropriate vocation and who think that they would stand a chance. As potential candidates, the selectorate may judge their electoral prospects to be doubtful and therefore may be reluctant to nominate them, even if they do not share the public's values (Bochel and Denver 1983). Lastly, in a direct way public attitudes could be reflected in the vote which female candidates attract, where considerations of gender override other factors like partisanship. This suggests that cultural attitudes might be significant, yet the matter is complex since countries which are often perceived as relatively traditional, such as Switzerland and Ireland, have double the number of women in office to the United States, where the second-wave women's movement might have been expected to have most impact on sex-role attitudes.

Alternative research suggests that a major role is played by *socio-economic factors*, especially the proportion of women in a country who are eligible for office by virtue of their economic and educational experience. The selectorate will only nominate candidates for office who have certain qualifications, increasingly requiring formal educational credentials. As a number of studies have found university qualifications distinguish élites from non-élites throughout the world (Putnam 1976; Blondel 1973; Loewenberg and Patterson 1979). Compared with the population, university graduates are statistically overrepresented in legislative élites, roughly ten or twenty to one (Putnam 1976). Education, as well as qualifying candidates to be nominated in the eyes of the selectorate, might also be important in motivating candidates to stand. Numerous cross-cultural studies have found that people with higher levels of education tend to participate more than others (Verba, Nie and Kim 1971; Almond and Verba 1963; Lipset 1960; Inkeles 1969; Milbraith and Goel 1977). Education leads to greater participation for many reasons. It is argued that the more educated are more likely to follow current affairs in the media, to acquire more information about government, to feel confident discussing political issues and to feel capable of influencing government. These greater feelings of political competence and efficacy lead the more educated to take an active role in electoral campaigning, community affairs and standing for office. This suggests that as the socio-economic experience of women changes they will gain the necessary qualifications which lead to positions in political élites.

Certain studies also suggests a significant connection between female recruitment and patterns of employment. Political élites tend to be dominated by representatives from a small number of occupational groups, particularly professionals. Lawyers are politically prominent almost everywhere; they usually make up 15 to 25 per cent of national legislators, rising to half of all representatives in America (Putnam 1976; Davidson and Oleszek 1981). Journalists, academics, teachers and businessmen are also overrepresented in parliaments compared with their numbers in the population (Loewenberg and Patterson 1979; Blondel 1973). These groups often lend practitioners skills which are useful in elected office, such as expertise and confidence in public speaking, knowledge of government and familiarity with the law. These jobs also allow considerable flexibility so that professionals can combine a long-term career with the demands and uncertainties of office, while this may be more difficult for workers in manual jobs or middle management. Elected office can be complementary rather than antithetical to the careers of many professionals. To have experience of the political world gives lawyers, businessmen and journalists a range of contacts which are useful in private practice. The high status of these jobs may influence selectorates when choosing candidates (Mezey 1979). For all these reasons representatives tend to be drawn disproportionately from professional groups. In so far as there are few women in these occupations, they are at a clear disadvantage in standing for office under present circumstances. As increasing numbers of women enter such professions as law, the media and business, this may place more on the traditional ladder leading to political office.

A further connection between employment and political participation is suggested by studies of campaign activists in the United States. Research has shown that female participation in politics is greatest among those women who work outside the home (Anderson 1975; Welch 1977). Employed women develop a greater interest in politics, and they might also develop stronger feelings of confidence and independence through their jobs, which leads to a sense of political efficacy. Work also offers the organisational basis for political activity through trade unions and business groups. On this basis more women in the workforce might lead to a greater number of motivated and well-connected female candidates willing to stand for office, if socio-economic factors are important.

Alternatively, others emphasise the significance of *political factors*, with the parties playing a crucial role as 'gatekeepers' to office. One of the primary functions of political parties is to nominate and support suitable candidates for office. If Socialist parties are committed to increasing sexual equality, then we would expect to find more women promoted by these parties as parliamentary representatives and party leaders. In an early study comparing France, West Germany, Norway and Italy, Duverger suggested that the most important variation in the number of women candidates is related to the nature of the political parties concerned, with the left-wing and the Christian parties giving women a better chance (Duverger 1955: 82). In a more recent comparison, Mossuz-Lavau and Sineau also support the view that in most European countries there is a greater inclination of the Left to admit women among its elected members: 'While in Scandinavia all parties are making the same effort to give women genuine political power, in the rest of Europe the left provides far more opportunities for women than other political parties' (Mossuz-Lavau and Sineau 1984). Further if we look at changes over time, this research suggests that left-wing parties blazed the trail for women in parliament, with other parties following in later years. In Italy, for example, in the three decades following the Second World War over half of all women elcted to the National Assembly and Senate were from the Communist Party (see Beckwith 1984). Other studies, however, conclude that the parties of the Left are not necessarily more likely to promote female candidates, in Sweden (Foverskov) and Britain (Rasmussen 1983). It is argued that the British Labour Party was less likely than Conservatives to nominate women for tactical reasons; they did not want to jeopardise their chances of winning seats by alienating voters (Rasmussen 1983). Therefore, we need to see in a range of countries whether women are more successful in Socialist parties and the significance of this in the context of institutional, cultural and socio-economic factors.

Alternatively, amongst political variables a number of recent studies stress the importance of voting systems, arguing that elections with proportional representation using the party list system give women a stronger chance of being nominated and elected than simple majority systems (Bogdanor 1981, 1984; Castles 1981; Rule 1981, 1984; Currell 1974; Kohn 1980); Lovenduski and Hills 1981; Krauss 1974; Means 1972; Duverger 1955). This is supported by evidence which shows that countries with first-past-the-post systems, such as Canada and Britain, have only a handful of women in parliament, while female representation is generally stronger in countries using proportional representation. Yet it is unclear why there are significant differences between countries which share a similar electoral system such as Belgium and Denmark or Israel and the Netherlands. It is also unclear how far the introduction of proportional representation would by itself improve the political position of women. As a recent study concluded:

May it be inferred, then, that proportional representation is invariably favourable to the choice of women as candidates and to their election to parliament? By no means. It may be seen . . . that among the countries which employ this system, the proportion of women in the lower chamber ranges from 29.2% (in Sweden) to 5.6% (in Belgium). In any event, the voting system is but one factor among several which can promote or impede the entry of women into elected assemblies. (Mossuz-Lavau and Sineau 1984)

This suggests the need to analyse the relative influence of voting systems compared with other factors as elections only function within a broader context.

We can directly compare the position of women in Socialist parties, and then go on to analyse the relative influence of environmental and political variables in a causal model using multiple regression. To analyse the electoral variables, countries were classified as party-list electoral systems or those which were nearer to majoritarian elections including first-past-the-post, alternative-vote and single-transferable-vote systems (Butler, Penniman and Ranney 1981). Cultural factors were assessed using a comparative political-egalitarianism index created from the EuroBarometer 1977 survey.[2] Data for this poll was drawn from 8,791 selected respondents in the nine member states of the European Community. Respondents were asked a series of items to gauge their attitudes towards the role of women and men. From these, four questions were selected to create an index measuring beliefs in political equality of the sexes in local, national and the European parliaments, including the items given in Table 6.2. While the EuroBarometer poll does not cover all the countries in the comparison it is the most extensive cross-cultural poll currently available. In addition, as an alternative measure of cultural differences the strength of Catholicism in each country was compared, on the expectation that Protestant countries would be less traditional in the roles expected of women. Lastly, to assess the impact of socio-economic variables, comparisons were made with the proportion of women in the labour force, in professional occupations such as lawyers, teachers and journalists and in the college population, as defined earlier.

Table 6.2: Political-egalitarian Index

Item	Positive egalitarian response (%)								
	Belg	Den	W. Ger	Fr	Ire	It	Lux	Neth	UK
If there were more women on your local council, would things go better or worse? [Better]	63	81	66	70	74	55	46	71	71
In National Parliament, if there were distinctly more women, do you think things would go better or worse? [Better]	64	81	67	70	77	52	48	74	69
In general, would you have more confidence in a man or a woman as your representative in Parliament? [Woman]	53	71	52	61	46	49	42	63	52
For the European Parliament, do you think it desirable or not that there should be quite a lot of women elected? [Desirable]	39	42	44	57	50	35	35	35	52
Average egalitarian score*	33	54	33	47	35	8	7	39	36

Note: * Pro-egalitarian minus anti-egalitarian response.
Source: EuroBarometer Poll, Oct./Nov. 1977 (EC).

CONCLUSIONS

Do Socialist parties, in accordance with their egalitarian ideology, directly improve the position of women within their own ranks? A comparison of national parliaments suggests that the Left does provide more opportunities for females in politics (Fig. 6.3); women are more strongly represented in Socialist parties in nearly all the countries under comparison. Over a quarter of the Social Democratic/ Labour members of parliament were women in Norway, Sweden and the Netherlands, and over a fifth of the parliamentary Communist parties were women in Portugal, Italy, Sweden and Belgium. Left-wing parties tend to provide more opportunities for women; however, this generalisation needs to be qualified as in some countries, including Greece, Britain and Austria, the differences between parties seems fairly marginal

Although from the above data parties seem to play an important role as 'gatekeepers' for women in politics, the question remains how significant this is compared with other factors such as the electoral system in use or the attitudes of voters towards female candidates. Given that the extent of female representation is a consequence of an extremely complex interaction of political, institutional, cultural and socio-economic factors, we need to establish the relative significance of each of these variables in a causal model.

If we compare the influence of all variables on women in legislatures, using multiple regression, it becomes clear that the role of parties is crucial. In particular, as shown in Figure 6.4, it seems that right-wing parties tend to act as the major barrier to female representation. Few women have gained access to legislative office in countries where the Right have dominated parliament ($r = 0.66$), whilst the association is reversed where the Left have been stronger ($r = 0.30$). This suggests that opportunities for women in politics can be significantly restricted or expanded by party selectorates. The results are significant since in many ways they represent the strictest test of the thesis that politics matters. The model confirms that Socialist parties have improved the position of women in the area where they

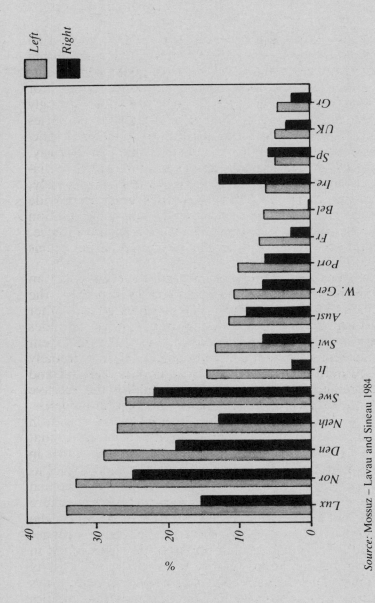

Figure 6.3 : Women in parliamentary parties

Source: Mossuz – Lavau and Sineau 1984

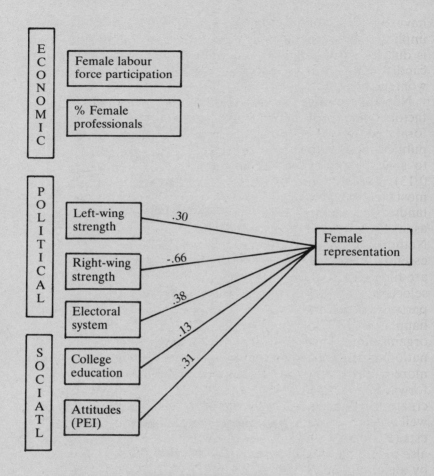

Note: Since this model is restricted to a single dependent variable, estimates are based on multiple linear regression. Stepwise selection was used checking for multicollinearities. Only statistically significant relationships are reported (p=>0.05). R2=0.98.

Figure 6.4 : Causal model of political equality

have the most direct influence, within their own ranks. It implies that the small number of women in political élites is due less to the shortage of women qualified to stand as candidates than to the party selectorate failing to nominate women for office.

Not that parties act in isolation, however, and other factors which proved significant included whether the electoral system was proportional or majoritarian (r = 0.38), public attitudes towards women in politics (r = 0.31) and, to a lesser extent, the educational status of women (r = 0.13). The influence of electoral systems can be explained most clearly by looking at how elections work in the Netherlands as an example of strict proportionality and in Britain as a pure majoritarian system. In countries such as the Netherlands there is one national constituency, and voters essentially choose between party lists of candidates. Seats are then allocated in exact proportion to votes. Rather than selecting individual representatives the voter is choosing a party, with a certain group of candidates, some of which happen to be women. Under this system, central party organisations have considerable influence over the nomination of candidates, and if they are committed to including more women, they have that option. As parties want to put forward an attractive slate of candidates, they will try to create a balanced ticket by including women and men, as well as all major regional, cultural, social and religious interests (Bogdanor 1981). In some systems women's groups can also manipulate these lists to their advantage, as in Norway, by deleting men's names on an organised basis so that women rise to a more favourable position within the party list (As 1984; Skaard 1981). There are many varieties of proportional representation as countries differ in such matters as the size and number of constituencies, but it is party-list systems which seem most favourable to women rather than multi-member constituencies (Castles 1981; see also Butler 1981 and Carstairs 1980).

In contrast, all the countries with low female representation use electoral systems nearer to the majoritarian type. Britain can be seen as an example of the first-past-the-post system where voters in a constituency chose a single candidate to represent them in Parliament. Under this system, although parties are very important, there is relatively more emphasis on individual candidates. There is closer scrutiny of the candidate's abilities, talents, experience, record, policies and personal characteristics. Gender differences can therefore play a more significant role as voters chose individual candidates rather than party lists. In addition, in Britain if the central parties wanted to include more female candidates, it would be difficult for the executive to impose its wishes on the local selectorates. The choice of candidates is in the hands of local parties who defend their independence in this matter. This means that any sort of quota system, to ensure that a certain percentage of candidates were women, would be very difficult to implement.

The influence of the electoral system is further confirmed by trends in particular countries. In Japan the highest number of female representatives was achieved in 1946 (7.6 per cent of members of the House of Representatives), but the number was cut in half the following year when the electoral system became less proportional. The same is true in France with the voting reforms in 1957. It is notable that France was also the country where there was the greatest contrast between the proportion of women in its national assembly (4.3 in 1979) and in its European delegation (21 per cent in 1979). For its 1979 national elections it used a two-ballot majority system in single-member constituencies, while for the European elections it used proportional representation with one country-wide constituency (Herman and Hagger 1980). The differences which voting systems produce in a simultaneous election can be seen most clearly in West Germany. Half the representatives are chosen by majoritarian single-member districts and the rest by *land* lists, but the vast majority of female members of the Bundestag (80 per cent) enter by the latter route (Kohn 1980).

Although electoral factors were significant, cultural attitudes also proved important; favourable attitudes towards female candidates had a positive influence on the number of women in office. The relative importance of these factors can be illustrated by the case of Switzerland, where women have greatly increased in national office under proportional representation despite the prevalence of traditional attitudes. That Switzerland is highly traditional in its attitudes can be shown in various ways. Switzerland was the last major European country to give women the national vote, in 1971, when women were also first allowed to stand for the Nationalrat and Standerat. Resistance to the principle still exists; in 1982 male citizens in one canton voted in the assembly to deny women the vote in local elections (Flanz 1983). In another indicator in a recent cross-national poll by Gallup, a third of the Swiss respondents agreed with the traditional idea that the male should be the breadwinner while the women stayed home to look after the house, which was a higher proportion than all the countries polled except Japan (Hastings 1980). Yet despite the predominence of conservative attitudes towards women's role, in the first national election for which Swiss women could stand in 1971, under proportional representation 5 per cent of those elected to the Nationalrat were women, which increased to 7.5 per cent in 1975 and 10.5 per cent in 1979. This is double the number of women in public office to countries like America, Canada and Britain with much more favourable attitudes towards women in politics, a longer tradition of female participation and stronger women's movements pressing for political equality.

Lastly, this analysis found that socio-economic factors, the position of women in the workforce, in the professions and in college, did not have a major influence on the number of women in office. That education and employment are relatively unimportant is shown most clearly by countries such as Canada and the United States, both of which have always had a high proportion of women in college and in work, although there have never been many women in politics in these countries. This suggests that even if women are making breakthroughs in other areas, rising in management, administration and the professions, gaining better qualifications and experience thought suitable for office, this does not imply that there will be similar progress in politics. As the 'gatekeepers' to public power, unless party selectorates are willing to nominate female candidates, placing them in winnable positions on party lists or in individual constituencies, then political inequalities will continue irrespective of other socio-economic trends.

7 Cultural Attitudes Towards Sexual Equality

The social indicators developed so far allow us to compare the material conditions of sexual stratification, but this leaves out of the analysis the ideological dimension of change: how women and men perceive gender roles. Yet some might argue that the women's movement has been more successful in changing attitudes towards sexual equality than the material conditions of women's lives. Since the 1960s there has been a substantial expansion of feminist culture with the proliferation of feminist literature, the creation of women's theatre and art groups, the development of feminist theory, the introduction of a women's studies perspective into many traditional academic disciplines and the successful establishment of feminist publishing houses and bookshops. Consciousness-raising small-group work to transform social attitudes towards gender roles has always been a central aspect of the women's movement. We therefore need to compare countries to see where attitudes towards sexual equality remain most traditional and to consider the implications of this for a model of social change.

MEASURES OF ATTITUDES TOWARDS WOMEN

The cross-cultural study of attitudes towards women raises the problem that frequently survey data cannot be compared between countries or over time. National surveys often have specific questions to gauge public opinion towards 'women's issues', included in such sources as the Gallup Report International (1980) or the Index to International Public Opinion (Hastings 1980), but they rarely include a wide range of consistent indicators such as those used in the Attitudes Towards Women Scale developed by Spence and Helmreich (Spence and Helmreich 1972; Beere 1979; Clarey, Norris and Smyth 1984). As well as the limitations of data, serious theoretical difficulties are raised by the comparison of public opinion in different cultures (Dogan and Pelassy 1984). Concepts such as 'the women's movement', 'women's liberation' or 'feminism' will have different connotations in different societies. Women may support the idea of reducing sexual stratification and yet not identify themselves as 'feminists' or as adherents of 'the women's movement'.

Bearing in mind these qualifications, the most thorough data which is available for comparison is provided in the EuroBarometer surveys on European women and men. These were carried out on behalf of the European Commission in the member states of the European Community in 1975, 1977 and 1983 with over 9,000 respondents in each survey.[1] This series includes a range of items designed to measure two aspects of attitudes towards sexual stratification: judgements about the *ideal* division of gender roles and perceptions about the *actual* extent of sexual equality. Since these surveys are limited to ten European countries, secondary comparisons are also drawn from the 1982 survey carried out for the UN Decade of Women in West Germany, Japan, the United States, Sweden and Britain.[2] These surveys do not include all the Western democracies compared in earlier chapters, but they provide the most comprehensive cross-national sources available in recent years. On the basis of an analysis of attitudes towards ideal gender-roles in the family, the workplace and political life, we can develop a classification of countries along the liberal–traditional continuum.

IDEAL SOCIAL, ECONOMIC AND POLITICAL GENDER ROLES

Given the emphasis of the women's movement on sharing responsibilities within the family, how far have social attitudes changed over the years? What is the ideal family in different societies? In the 1983 EuroBarometer respondents were given a choice of the ideal division of roles within the family, from the alternatives of a family where the two partners each have an equally absorbing job and where housework and the care of children are shared equally between them (egalitarian) to a family where the wife has a less demanding job than her husband and where she does the larger share of the housework and caring for children (moderate), and lastly a family where only the husband has a job and the wife runs the home (traditional).

As Figure 7.1 shows, overall public opinion was fairly evenly divided between the ideal family types, with about a third in favour of the most egalitarian relationships. There were marked contrasts in different societies, however, with Greece, Denmark, Italy and France emerging as the most liberal, while Luxembourg, Belgium and Ireland were the most traditional. As one might expect, within EC countries attitudes also varied by gender and age, with over half of the younger group (15–24 years) in favour of equality compared with only a quarter of the older respondents (55 years and over). While not strictly comparable, in the United Nations survey there was a similar item asking respondents whether they were in favour or against the idea that the husband should work outside the home and the wife should keep house. Responses again showed substantial cross-sectional contrasts. Amongst the Japanese, 72 per cent favoured the traditional view compared with 34 per cent in the United States, 33 per cent in West Germany, 26 per cent in Britain and 14 per cent in Sweden. Therefore, although the view of women as full-time housewives may have changed over the years, in the 1980s a substantial proportion still hold to traditional values, especially amongst the older generation.

Have expectations of gender roles changed more radically

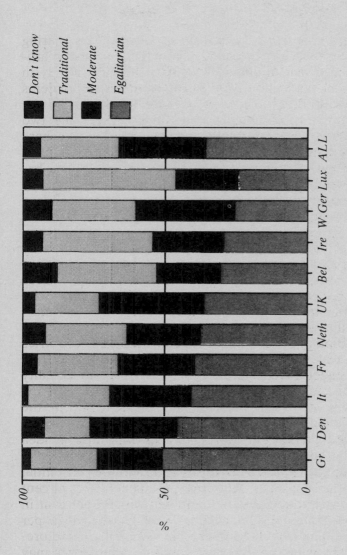

Legend: Don't know, Traditional, Moderate, Egalitarian

Source: EuroBarometer 1983

Figure 7.1 : Ideal division of family roles

in employment? Have values become more liberal as a result of the increasing numbers of women entering the labour market? Or do social attitudes still restrict women to a limited range of 'pink-collar' jobs? The 1983 EuroBarometer survey asked a series of questions which were designed to measure the extent of role stereotyping in employment by asking respondents whether they had more confidence in a man or a women in certain predominantly male occupations, such as a lawyer, surgeon or train driver (traditional), or equal confidence in both sexes (egalitarian). Generally, over half of the respondents felt that men and women were equally appropriate for the occupations, although about a third were traditionalists who felt that they had more confidence in a man as a driver, surgeon, lawyer or member of parliament and in a woman as a doctor delivering a baby. Except for the latter job, very few (>6 per cent) expressed more confidence in a women in any category. However, there were significant differences of opinion cross-culturally (Fig. 7.2) with the most consistent egalitarian attitudes across all occupations in Denmark, France and the Netherlands and, at the other extreme, the most traditional attitudes expressed in Greece and Italy. Further, the differences between countries were greater than the differences by gender, age or education, although all of these factors had some effect on traditional attitudes in the expected direction.

The 1983 EuroBarometer also attempted to gauge perceptions of the actual position of women at work, to see whether they were thought to be treated equally. As might be expected given the economic inequalities outlined in Chapter 4, the results showed that half of all respondents recognised that the position of women was worse than men in terms of their pay, promotion prospects and the range of jobs open to them, although most felt that there was equality in training and job security. Cross-culturally, *perceptions* of economic inequalities were strongest in West Germany, Denmark and France, although as we have seen these are not the countries where the *actual* sex differentials were greatest in terms of pay or occupational segregation. Many women were also aware that these inequalities had a direct bearing on their own working lives: over half of all

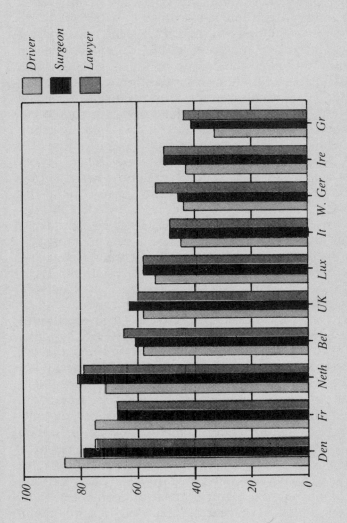

Source: EuroBarometer 1983

Figure 7.2 : Equal confidence in both sexes for work

men (57 per cent) but only a quarter of all women (27 per cent) thought that their sex tended to be an advantage to their employment.

Lastly, what were perceptions of ideal gender-roles in the political dimension of equality? Do most people today support a greater involvement of women in public life or do traditional values continue to prevail? The EuroBarometer included a series of items on attitudes towards female participation in public office, some of which were outlined in the last chapter. In terms of perceptions of the most appropriate sex roles in politics, respondents were asked whether they agreed or disagreed that politics should be left to men. As Figure 7.4 shows, most respondents rejected this idea, with only minor differences between women and men. The results also suggest that over the last few years there has been a notable shift of opinion towards more egalitarian views: in 1975, 41 per cent of all respondents disapproved of the idea that politics should be left to men compared with almost three-quarters (72 per cent) in 1983. Traditional attitudes remained strong, however, in certain countries, including West Germany, Belgium, Ireland and Luxembourg, and similar cross-national variations were evident in other items on political equality, including confidence in a woman as a member of parliament.

Are there any systematic patterns to explain cross-cultural differences in attitudes? To analyse where women give strongest support to some central aims of the women's movement we can construct a general index including support for sexual equality in gender roles, in social attitudes, in the workplace, in political life and in sharing childcare.[2] On the basis of this index we can suggest that, overall, the surveys demonstrated overwhelming support for sexual equality (Table 7.1), especially in the economic and political dimensions. Almost nine out of ten women agreed with the aims of equality at work and in political élites. Liberal attitudes amongst women vary cross-nationally, although the differences were not sharply polarised. As we might expect given the cultural influence of Catholicism, Ireland, Italy and the Netherlands emerged as some of the more traditional societies using these measures, although attitudes were least favourable towards equality in Britain. In order

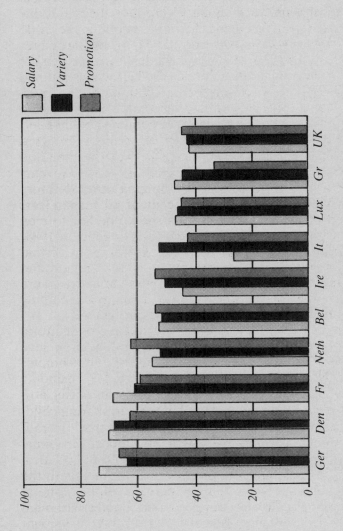

Q. Compared with men, is the present situation of working women better or worse?

Figure 7.3 : Perceptions of economic inequality

to consider these cross-national differences in more depth we need to go on to develop a classificatory typology based on the relationship between social attitudes and material conditions, and then to discuss the implications of this for the women's movement.

Table 7.1: Gender equality index amongst women (% agree)*

	Equal roles	Equal attitudes	Equality work	Equality politics	Equality child-care	Av.
Greece	83.9	81.7	89.0	83.7	89.1	85.5
France	81.0	83.4	89.7	88.7	75.5	83.8
Germany	77.1	81.8	89.8	87.1	74.8	82.1
Belgium	71.1	83.3	88.3	88.3	72.7	80.7
Denmark	73.3	57.4	92.8	93.1	87.9	80.9
Luxembourg	81.3	79.4	90.5	81.4	72.1	80.9
Ireland	76.2	77.9	88.9	89.9	66.0	79.8
Italy	68.8	79.8	84.2	80.3	74.7	77.6
Netherlands	66.9	56.5	86.2	85.7	69.4	72.9
UK	62.6	63.7	84.5	86.1	60.6	71.5
All	74.3	74.5	88.4	86.4	74.3	79.6

Note: *(See Note 2 for details).
Source: EuroBarometer 1983.

NOTES

1. The author would like to thank the ECPR and the authors of the EuroBarometer Surveys on European Women and Men for making the data available. The EuroBarometer surveys included the following number of adult respondents: N. 9,600 in 1983; N. 9,000 in 1979; N. 9,500 in 1975.
2. N. 6,271.
3. The items used for this index were as follows:
   Q.1. Do you agree or disagree with women who claim that there should be fewer differences between the respective roles of men and women in society? [Equal roles.]

   Q.2. There are many different movements and associations concerned with the situation of women and they vary in their specific aims. For each of the following would you tell me if you agree completely, agree to some extent, disagree to some extent or disagree completely with this aim?

   • Fight against prejudiced people who would like to keep women in a subordinate role to men both in the family and in society. [Equal attitudes.]

- Obtain true equality between women and men in their work and careers. [Economic equality.]

- Persuade the political parties to give women the same chances as men of reaching responsible positions in the parties and of becoming candidates for elections. [Political equality.]

- Arrange things so that when a child is unwell it could be either the father or the mother who stays at home to care for it. [Equal child-care.]

8 Conclusions: Sexual Stratification and Social Change

Today in many countries the women's movement seems to be on the defensive, facing increased opposition from the New Right and a harsher economic climate in the 1980s. Recently, organised feminism has been more intent on preserving established rights than successfully placing new issues on the political agenda. In the early 1970s the burgeoning women's movement mobilised widespread public support in a vigorous and diverse campaign for sexual equality. The creative activity during this period has left an enduring legacy, but feminism, in common with other mass movements, like the campaign for nuclear disarmament in Europe or the civil rights movement in the United States, experiences considerable fluctuations in support according to political and economic circumstances. Organised feminism remains an extraordinarily diverse and wider-ranging movement, with heterogeneous strategies, campaigns and tactics in different countries. Given this plurality of concerns, the comparative strength of organised feminism cannot be documented in a systematic way, but on the basis of the material presented in previous chapters we can develop a theoretical classification which divides societies into four ideal types depending on their material conditions and social attitudes (Fig. 8.1). Within this analytical typology we can extend the theory of relative deprivation to start to explain the strengths and weaknesses of the women's movement in different countries.

We can suggest that those societies which have experienced comparatively rapid progress in the position of women can be classified as egalitarian-liberal. Countries

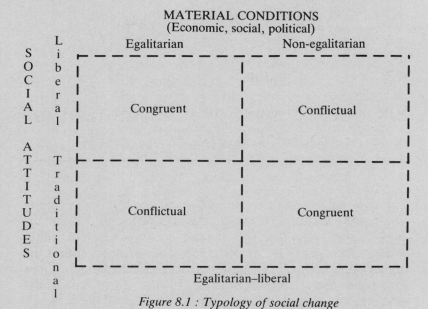

Figure 8.1 : Typology of social change

which fall into this group are characterised by lower levels of sexual stratification, with relatively few inequalities between women and men in the distribution of rewards, status and power, combined with predominately liberal attitudes towards sex roles. There is a congruent relationship between ideological values and social conditions. It can be suggested on the basis of the previous chapters that many Scandinavian countries exemplify this type of society. Sweden and Denmark, for example, rank as amongst the most equal according to most of the social, economic and political indicators we have compared, while in these countries the debate on sex roles has been high on the public agenda since the 1930s and the need for gender change to benefit both women and men has been widely accepted. This is not to claim that women and men have achieved absolute equality in these countries, only that women are nearer this goal in Sweden and Denmark than elsewhere. On this basis we would expect as a consequence that the women's movement in these countries would be consensual rather than conflictual, with a fairly low profile since many of their demands would be accepted by society as a whole.

NON-EGALITARIAN-LIBERAL

We can also suggest that in certain societies, such as the United States, one of the most striking phenomena is the marked contrast between the expectations and achievements of the women's movement. In North America social attitudes seem to have changed radically over the last decades so that women have relatively high expectations of gender change. In few other countries are women so conscious of gender inequalities, so articulate in asserting their rights and so well organised in representing their interests as a group. The women's movement in America has been at the forefront of the debate on gender change since the publication of seminal works such as Friedan's *The Feminine Mystique* (1964) and the founding of the National Organisation of Women (NOW) in the same year. As a result of liberal cultural traditions and the activities of organised feminism, it seems that today in the United States women have strongly egalitarian attitudes towards sex roles.

For many women in America, however, there seems to be a marked contradiction between conscious expectations and objective economic, political and social conditions. The average woman in the United States experiences considerable inequalities in her everyday life. The women's movement has been highly vocal in pressing for equal pay over the last twenty years, but as we have seen, the average pay-packet for full-time American women workers compared with that of men is lower than in almost all European countries. Many middle-class women have made impressive breakthroughs in management, administration and the professions, but at the same time there have been substantial increases in the number of women in low-paid, low-status 'pink collar' service jobs. Compared with countries in the European Community, America has one of the highest proportions of women in the labour force, but as we have outlined, their average wages are among the lowest. There has also been a substantial growth of the female 'nouveau poor' in the United States due to the relatively high divorce rate, the number of single-parent families and the less comprehensive and generous welfare system there (Scott

1984; Kamerman 1984; Norris 1984). In other ways, American women experience greater objective inequalities than exist in Europe. Despite hopes of political change there have been fewer women in the US Congress in recent years than in equivalent legislatures in almost all countries of the European Community. The same inequalities of power are found at other levels of government. As a result it seems that American women have relatively high expectations of sexual equality but they face relatively non-egalitarian objective conditions.

The net result of these contradictions may lead many women to be highly conscious of the relative deprivation experienced by women as a group. The concept of relative deprivation has been developed most extensively in relation to social class, but it can be applied to any social group (see Runciman 1966). It suggests that people's aspirations and grievances largely depend on their frame of reference. We might expect, for instance, that the better the salary and working conditions, in general the higher the level of job satisfaction, yet this might not necessarily be the case. A female company manager, for example, may be aggrieved if passed over for an appointment to the executive boardroom when she feels that she was as well qualified to be promoted as the person selected. On the other hand, a female secretary, with a lower pay packet than the manager, may be satisfied with her position if she had no higher ambitions and if she compares herself with women in the typing pool. The idea of relative deprivation suggests that a person feels a sense of deprivation in comparison with others rather than in comparison with any objective criteria. What triggers dissatisfaction is not the absolute conditions, such as low pay or status, but the expectation that conditions should be, and could be, equal to another reference group or individual. This means that material conditions may improve for women, ethnic minorities or the working class but if expectations rise faster then dissatisfaction may actually increase. Indeed, improving conditions may fuel expectations rather than dampen them down, by holding out the possibility of change.

The concept of relative deprivation implies that women will not be mobilised into political activity by the experience of the feminisation of poverty or increasing domestic violence or the lack of child-care facilities *per se*, rather it is when women become conscious of their inequality as a group relative to others in society that they will become dissatisfied. If women are not aware how gender influences their position in society, then the experience of social inequalities will not lead to political action since inequalities will seem natural and inevitable. Difficulties in combining a career with child-care, or coping with a violent spouse, or problems in surviving on welfare, or the lack of promotion prospects will seem to be personal problems facing the individual rather than systematic social inequalities shared by women as a group. Dissatisfaction with sexual stratification therefore depends on the difference between ideal gender-roles and actual conditions. If women in the United States are conscious of relative deprivation, aware of considerable conflict between their expectations and experience, then as a result we would expect women to be highly politicised as a group and articulate in demanding social change.

NON-EGALITARIAN-TRADITIONAL

In certain societies women face highly unequal economic and political conditions, including low wages, poor working conditions, restrictive practices, low status and little power. The concept of relative deprivation suggests that this experience by itself will not produce demands for social change unless women become aware of their relative position as a group. In non-egalitarian-traditional societies the position of the sexes is seen as inevitable, indeed as desirable, so that there is little pressure for radical reform. It can be suggested that countries such as Japan and Switzerland most clearly exemplify this congruent ideal type. Despite material conditions in non-egalitarian-traditional societies, we would expect the women's movement to receive little support and for feminists to be fairly quiescent as a pressure group.

EGALITARIAN-TRADITIONAL

Lastly, in some societies women may experience relatively egalitarian material conditions and yet have fairly traditional attitudes towards sex roles. Not many countries would be expected to fall into this category but it is theoretically possible that economic or social conditions could be in advance of public attitudes; for example, if a radical political élite tried to introduce positive discrimination measures or liberal abortion laws in advance of public opinion. As in other societies with traditional attitudes, we would not expect the women's movement to be well supported as an interest group.

At this stage this typology can only be considered to provide an analytical basis for classification, given the heterogeneous nature of the women's movement, it is not possible to test the applicability of the theory in a systematic way. Although the theory of relative deprivation remains speculative, it nevertheless seems to provide a fruitful framework for further comparative research into the strength of organised feminism in particular countries with interesting implications for the future of the women's movement. The theory suggests that to a large extent support for feminist activity will depend on the conflict between women's expectations and experiences. In mobilising for further action on matters like equal pay, positive discrimination or child-care facilities, the women's movement has to convince women not just that certain feminist goals are desirable but, above all, that they are attainable.

In assessing change over the last decades feminists have to steer a difficult course between the Scylla of complacency and the Charybdis of cynicism. On the one hand, some feel that the women's movement has become redundant as a result of its very success: what more could women want? Government resolutions and formal commitments to equal opportunities are taken as evidence of action. Now that a framework of legislation for equal rights is widely established it can be assumed complacently that 'things must be getting better', with the proviso that gradual change takes time. On the other hand, some are cynical about the possibilities of change, given the difficulties in reducing sexual stratification in political élites, occupational segregation or the division of roles within the family, despite the establishment of a range of policy measures over the last decades. In the cynical view it is assumed that gender roles, if not immutable, are at least largely unalterable in the short-term through political means. It is hoped that this comparative analysis, which has shown that there are significant cross-cultural differences in sexual stratification which are strongly related to political variables, helps to guard against both the overly cynical and the overly complacent perspectives.

References

Aberbach, J. D., Putnam, R. D. and Rockman, B. A. (1983) *Bureaucrats and Politicians in Western Democracies*, Harvard University Press, Cambridge, Mass.

Adams, C. T. and Winston, K. T. (1980) *Mothers At Work*, Longman, London.

Almond, G. A. and Coleman, J. S. (1960) *The Politics of Developing Areas*, Princeton University Press, Princeton.

Almond, G. A. and Verba, S. (1963) *The Civic Culture*, Princeton University Press, Princeton.

Alt, J. E. (1978) *The Politics of Economic Decline*, Cambridge University Press, Cambridge.

Anderson, K. (1975) 'Working women and political participation', in *American Journal of Political Science*, 19 (3), August, 439–53.

Andrews, A. (1982) 'Towards a Status of Women Index' *Professional Geographer*, 34 (1), February, 24–31.

As, B. (1984) 'Norway, more power to women' paper at the *Second International Congress on Women*, Groningen.

Ashworth, G. and Bonnerjea, L. (1985) *The Invisible Decades: UK Women in the UN Decade 1976–1985*, Gower, Aldershot.

Banks, A. S. (1971) *Cross-Polity Time Series Data* MIT Press, Cambridge, Mass.

Bashevkin, S. B. (ed.) (1985) *Women and Politics in Western Europe*, Frank Cass, London.

Beale, J. (1986) *Women in Ireland*, Macmillan, London.

Beckworth, K. (1984) 'Structural barriers to women's access to office', paper for the American Political Science Association Conference, Washington, D.C.

Beere, C. A. (1979) *Women and Women's Issues*, Jossey-Bass Press, San Francisco.

Bell, D. (1960) *The End of Ideology*, Free Press, Glencoe, Ill.

Benevia, L. (1982) *Women and Development*, Praeger, New York.

Berch, B. (1982) *The Endless Day*, Harcourt Brace Jovanovich, San Diego.

Berki, R. N. (1975) *Socialism*, Dent, London.

Blondel, J. (1973) *Comparative Legislatures*, Prentice Hall, New York.

Boaden, N. (1971) *Urban Policy-Making*, Cambridge University Press, Cambridge.

Bochel, J. and Denver, D. (1983), 'Candidate selection in the Labour party', in *British Journal of Political Science*, 13 (1), January, 45–69.

Bogdanor, V. (1981) *The People and the Party System*, Cambridge University Press, Cambridge.

Bogdanor, V. (1983) *What is Proportional Representation?*, Martin Robertson, Oxford.

Bouchier, D. (1983) *The Feminist Challenge*, Macmillan, London.

Boulding, E., Nuss, S. A., Carson, D. L. and Greenstein, M. A. (1976) *Handbook of International Data on Women*, Sage, Beverly Hills.

Boulding, E. (1977) *Women in the Twentieth Century World*, Sage, Beverly Hills.

Boutilier, L. (1970) *The Making of Political Women*, Nelson Hall, USA.

Bradshaw, J. (1982) *The Women's Liberation Movement*, Pergamon Press, Oxford.

Brekke, T. *et al.* (1985) *Women: A World Report*, Methuen, London.

Bristow, S. L. (1980) 'Women councillors: An explanation of the underrepresentation of women in local government', *Local Government Studies*, 6(3), May/June, 73–90.

Brooks, J. E. (1983) 'Left-wing mobilisation and socioeconomic equality', *Comparative Political Studies*, 16 (3), 393-416.

Buckley, M. and Anderson, M. (eds) (1987) *Women, Equality and Europe*, Macmillan, London.

Butler, D. E. and Stokes, D. (1974) *Political Change in Britain*, (2nd ed), Macmillan, London.

Butler, D., Penniman, H. and Ranney, A. (1981) *Democracy at the Polls*, AEI, Washington, D.C.

Cameron, D. R. (1978) 'The expansion of the public economy: a comparative analysis', *American Political Science Review* 72 (4) 1243–61.

Carley, M. (1981) *Social Measurement and Social Indicators*, Allen & Unwin, London.

Carstairs, A. M. (1980) *A Short History of Electoral Systems in Europe*, Allen & Unwin, London.

Castles, F. G. (1982) *The Impact of Parties*, Sage, London.

Castles, F. G. (1981) 'Female legislative representation and the electoral system', *Politics*, 1(3), 21–7.

Castles, F. G. and McKinley, R. (1979) 'Does politics matter?' *European Journal of Political Research* 7(2) 169–86.

Castles, F. G. (1978) *The Social Democratic Image of Society*, Routledge & Kegan Paul, London.

Caulfield, M. D. (1981) 'Equality, sex and mode of production' in G. D. Berreman (ed.), *Social Inequality*, Academic Press, New York.

CAWP (1984) 'Women in elective office: factsheet', Center for the American Women and Politics, Eagleton Institute of Politics, Rutgers University, New Jersey.

Cazes, B. (1972) 'The development of social indicators: a survey in A. Shonfield and S. Shaw (eds) *Social Indicators and Social Policy*, Heinemann, London.

Charvet, J. (1982) *Feminism*, Dent, London.

Christenson, R. M. *et al.* (1971) *Ideologies and Modern Politics*, Nelson, London.

Clarey, J., Norris, P., and Smyth, A. (1984) 'The post-feminist generation: a comparative study of Ireland, Britain and America', National Women's Studies Association Conference Paper, Seattle.

Collver, A. and Langlois, E. (1962) 'The female labor force in metropolitan areas: an international comparison', *Economic Development and Cultural Change*, 10 (4), July, 367–85.

Congress (1985) *Children in Poverty*, Congressional Research Service and Congressional Budget Office, Washington DC.

Cook, R. J. and Dickens, B. M. (1979) 'Abortion laws in Commonwealth Countries' *International Digest of Health Legislation*, 30(3), 395–502, World Health Organisation, Geneva.

Cook, A. H. (1975) *The Working Mother: A Survey of Problems and Programs in Nine Countries*, Cornell University Press, New York.

Crompton, R. and Mann, M. (eds) (1986) *Gender and Stratification*, Polity Press, Oxford.

Culley, M. and Portuges, C. (1985) *Gendered Subjects: The Dynamics of Feminist Teaching*, Routledge & Kegan Paul, London.

Currell, M. E. (1974) *Political Woman*, Croom Helm, Beckenham.

Cutright, P. (1965) 'Political structures, economic development and national social security programs', *American Journal of Sociology* 70 (5), March, 537–50.

Dahl, R. (1971) *Polyarchy: Participation and Opposition*, Yale University Press, New Haven, Conn.

Daly, M. (1978) *Gyn/Ecology: The Metaethics of Radicals Feminism*, Women's Press, London.

Darling, M. (1975) *The Role of Women in the Economy: A Summary Based on Ten National Reports*, OECD, Paris.

Davidson, R. and Oleszek, W. T. (1981) *Congress and its Members*, Congressional Quarterly Press, Washington D.C.

Dawson, R. E. and Robinson, J. A. (1963) 'Interparty competition, economic variables and welfare policies in the American states' *Journal of Politics* 25 (2), May, 265–89.

Davis, K. (1949) *Human Society*, Macmillan, New York.

Day, A. J. and Degenhardt, H. W. (1980) *Political Parties of the World*, Longman, London.

De Beauvoir, S. (1984) 'France: feminism—alive, well, and in constant danger' in Morgan, R. *Sisterhood is Global*, Anchor Press, New York.

Deutsch, K. W. (1980) 'On the utility of indicator systems' in C. L. Taylor (ed.) *Indicator Systems for Political, Economic and Social Analysis*, Oelgeschlager, Boston.

Diamond, I. (ed.) (1983) *Families, Political and Public Policy*, Longman, New York.

Dixon, R. B. (1976) 'Measuring equality between the sexes' in *Journal of Social Issues* 32 (3), 19–32.

Dogan, M. and Pelassy, D. (1984) *How to Compare Nations*, Chatham, Chatham, New Jersey.

Dryzek, J. (1978) 'Politics, economics and inequality: a cross-national analysis', *European Journal of Political Research* 6 (4), Dec, 399–410.

Duchen, C. (1986) *Feminism in France*, Routledge & Kegan Paul, London.

Duverger, M. (1955) *The Political Role of Women*, UNESCO, Paris.

Dye, T. (1966) *Politics, Economics & the Public: Policy Outcomes in the American States*, Rand McNally, Chicago.

Dye, T. R. (1976) *Policy Analysis*, University of Alabama Press, Alabama.

Ehrenreich, B. and Stallard, K. (1982) 'The nouveau poor', *MS* July/August.

Eichler, M. (1980) *The Double Standard*, Croom Helm, London.

Eisenstein, H. (1984) *Contemporary Feminist Thought*, Allen & Unwin, London.

Elshtain, J. B. (1981), *Public Man, Private Woman*, Princeton University Press, Princeton, NJ.

Engels, F. (1884) *The Origins of the Family, Private Property and the State*

Epstein, C. F. and Coser, R. L. (eds) (1981) *Access to Power: Crossnational Studies of Women and Elites*, Allen & Unwin, London.

Erikson, R. S. (1978) 'The relationship between public opinion and state policy: A new look based on some forgotten data', *American Journal of Political Science* 20(1) Feb, 25–26.

European Commission (1983) *Community Law and Women*, Women of Europe Supplement No. 12, Commission, Brussels.

European Commission (1982) *One-Parent Families and Poverty in the EEC*, EC, Copenhagen, December.

EuroStat (1984) *Social Indicators for the European Community*, European Commission, Brussels.

Ferber, M. A. and Lowry, H. M. (1977) 'Woman's place: national differences in the occupational mosaic', *Journal of Marketing* 41 (3) July, 23–30.

Ferriss, A. L. (1971) *Indicators of Trends in the Status of American Women*, Russell Sage, New York.

Field, M. J. (1979) 'Determinants of abortion policy in the developed nations', *Policy Studies Journal* 7 (4) Summer, 771–81.

Firestone, S. (1971) *The Dialectic of Sex*, Cape, London.

Flanz, G. H. (1983) *Comparative Women's Rights and Political Participation in Europe*, Transnational, New York.

Francome, C. (1984) *Abortion Freedom: A Worldwide Movement*, Allen & Unwin, London.

Friedan, B. (1963) *The Feminine Mystique*, W. W. Norton, New York.

Fry, B. R. and Winters, R. F. (1970) 'The politics of redistribution', *American Political Science Review* 64 (2), June, 508–22.

Galenson, M. (1973) *Women and Work: An International Comparison*, New York State School of Industrial and Labour Relations, New York.

Gelb, J. and Palley, M. L. (1983) *Women and Public Policies*, Princeton University Press, Princeton, N. J.

Giele, J. Z. and Smock, A. C. (1977) *Women: Roles and Status in Eight Countries*, Wiley, New York.

Goldberg, S. (1977) *The Inevitability of Patriarchy*, Temple Smith, London.

Gough, I. (1979) *The Political Economy of the Welfare State*, Macmillan, London.

Haavio-Mannila *et al.* (1985) *Unfinished Democracy: Women in Nordic Politics*, Pergamon Press, Oxford.

Hakim, C. (1979) *Occupational Segregation*, Department of Employment, Research Paper No. 9 HMSO.

Hastings, E. H. and Hastings, P. K. (1980) *Index to International Public Opinion 1978–79*, Greenwood Press, Westport.

Heclo, H. (1974) *Modern Social Politics in Britain and Sweden*, Yale University Press, New Haven, Conn.

Hewitt, C. (1977) 'The effect of political democracy and social democracy on equality in industrial societies: a cross national comparison', *American Sociological Review* 42 (3) June, 450–64.

Herman, V. and Hagger, M. (1980) *The Legislation of Direct Elections to the European Parliament*, Gower, Aldershot.

Hibbs, D. A. (1977) 'Political parties and macroeconomic policy', *American Political Science Review* 71 (4), Dec. 1467–87.

Hofferbert, R. I. (1966) 'The relation between public policy and some structural and environmental variables in the American States', *American Political Science Review* 60 (1) March, 73–82.

Iglitzin, L. B. and Ross, R. (1978) *Women in the World: A Comparative Study*, Clio, Oxford.

Inkeles, A. (1969) 'Participant citizenship in six developing countries', *American Political Science Review* 63(4), Dec, 1120–41.

International Labour Organisation (Annual) *Yearbook of Labour Statistics*, ILO, Geneva.

International Labour Office (1985) *Women at Work* 1, ILO, Geneva.

Jackman, R. W. (1980) 'Socialist parties and income inequalities in Western industrial societies', *Journal of Politics* 42(1) Feb, 135/149.

Joreskog, K. G. and Sorbom, D. (1983) *Lisrel IV Users Guide*, University of Uppsala, Sweden.

Kamerman, S. B. (1984) 'Women, children, and poverty: public policies and female-headed families in industrialised countries', *Signs* 10(2), Winter, 249/71.

Kamerman, S. B. and Kahn, A. J. (1978) *Family Policy: Government and Families in Fourteen Countries*, Columbia University Press, New York.

Kavanagh, D. (1983) *Political Science and Political Behaviour*, Ch. 6, Allen & Unwin, London.

Kerr, C. *et al.* (1960) *Industrialism and Industrial Man*, Harvard University Press, Cambridge, Mass.

King, A. (1981) 'What do elections decide?' in D. Butler, H. R. Penniman and A. Ranney (eds) *Democracy at the Polls*, AEI, Washington, D.C.

Klein, R. (1976) 'The politics of public expenditure: American theory and British practice', *British Journal of Political Science* 6 (4), Oct, 401–432.

Klein, V. (1963) 'Industrialisation and the changing role of women', *Current Sociology* 12, 24/34.

Kohn, W. S. (1980) *Women in National Legislatures*, Praeger, New York.

Krauss, W. R. (1974) 'Political implications of gender roles', *American Political Science Review* 68 (4), Dec, 1706–23.

Langland, E. and Gove, W. (1981) *A Feminist Perspective in the Academy*, University of Chicago Press, Chicago.

Lijphart, A. (1984) *Democracies*, Yale University Press, New Haven.

Liljestrom, R. (1984) 'Sweden: similarity, singularity and sisterhood' in R. Morgan (ed.) *Sisterhood in Global*, Anchor Press, New York.

Lipset, S. M. (1960) *Political Man*, Doubleday, New York.

Loewenberg, G. and Patterson, S. C. (1979) *Comparing Legislatures*, Little Brown, Boston.

Lovenduski, J. and Hills, J. (1981) *The Politics of the Second Electorate*, Routledge & Kegan Paul, London.

Lovenduski, J. and Outshoorn, J. (1986) *The New Politics of Abortion*, Sage, London.

Lovenduski, J. (1986) *Women and European Politics*, Wheatsheaf Books, Brighton.

Mackie, T. T. and Rose, R. (1982) *The International Almanac of Electoral History* (2nd ed), Macmillan, London.

Matsell, C. (1981) 'Spain' in Lovenduski and Hills (1981).

Matthiasson, C. J. (1974) *Many Sisters: Women in Cross-Cultural Perspective*, Free Press, New York.

Mead, M. (1981) *Male and Female*, Harmondsworth, Middx.

Means, I. N. (1972) 'Political recruitment of women in Norway', *Western Political Quarterly* 25(3), September, 491–521.

Mezey, M. L. (1979 *Comparative Legislatures*, Duke University Press, USA.

Meehan, E. M. (1985) *Women's Rights at Work*, Macmillan, London.

Milbraith, L. W. and Goel, M. L. (1977) *Political Participation*, 2nd edn, Rand McNally, Chicago.

Milburn, J. (1976) *Women as Citizens: A Comparative Review*.

Mill, J. S. (1869) *The Subjection of Women*.

Millett, K. (1971) *Sexual Politics*, Hart-Davis, London.

Mitchell, J. J. (1971) *Women's Estate*, Harmondsworth, Middx.

Mitchell, J. J. (1975) *Psychoanalysis and Feminism*, Harmondsworth, Middx.

Morgan, R. (ed.) (1984) *Sisterhood is Global*, Anchor Press, New York.

Morgan, R. (ed.) (1977) *Sisterhood is Powerful*, Vintage, New York.

Mossuz-Lavau, J. and Sineau, M. (1984) *The Situation of Women in the Political Process in Europe*, Council of Europe, Strasbourg.

Nelson, C. and Olesen, V. (1977) 'Veil and illusion: a critique of the concept of equality in western thought', *Catalyst* 10–11.

Newland, K. (1979) *The Sisterhood of Man*, Norton, New York.

Norris, P. (1984) *Women in poverty: Britain and America, Social Policy* 14 (4) (Spring), 41–43.

Norris, P. (1985) 'The Gender Gap: America and Britain', *Parliamentary Affairs* 38(2) Spring, 192/201.

Norris, P. (1986) 'Conservative attitudes in recent British elections: an emerging gender gap?', *Political Studies* 34(1) March, 18–26.

Norris, P. (1986) 'Women in Congress: a policy difference?', *Politics* 6(1), 34–40.

Oakley, A. and Oakley, R. (1979) 'Sexism in Official Statistics' in J. Irvine (ed.) *Demystifying Social Statistics*, Pluto, London.

OECD (1980) *Women and Employment*, OECD, Paris.

OECD, (1982) *The OECD List of Social Indicators*, OECD, Paris.

OECD (1985) *The Integration of Women into the Economy*, OECD, Paris.

Oppenheimer, V. K. (1973) 'Demographic influence on female employment and the status of women', *American Journal of Sociology* 78, 946–61.

Outshoorn, J. (1985) 'The politics of abortion in European States' in M. Buckley and M. Anderson (1987).

Patai, R. (ed.) (1967) *Women in the Modern World*, Free Press, New York.

Paterson, P. (1967) *The Selectorate*, MacGibbon and Kee, London.

Parkin, F. (1971) *Class Inequality and Political Order*, MacGibbon and Kee, London.

Parsons, T. (1970) 'Equality and inequality in modern society', *Social Inquiry* 40 (Spring), 13–72.

Pearce, D. (1979) 'Women, work and welfare: the feminisation of poverty' in K. W. Feinstein (ed.) *Working Women and Families*, Sage, London.

Powell, G. B. (1982) *Contemporary Democracies*, Harvard University Press, Cambridge, Mass.

Powers, M. F. (1982) *Measures of Socioeconomic Status: Current Issues*, AAAS Selected Symposium 81, Westview, Boulder, Co.

Przeworski, A. and Teune, H. (1970) *The Logic of Comparative Social Enquiry*, John Wiley, London.

Putnam, R. D. (1976) *The Comparative Study of Political Elites*, Prentice Hall, Eaglewood Cliffs, NJ.

Rasmussen, J. (1983) 'Women's role in contemporary British politics: impediments to parliamentary candidates', *Parliamentary Affairs* 36(3), 300–15.

Ratner, R. S. (1980) *Equal Employment Policy for Women*. Temple University Press, Philadelphia, PA.

Rein, M. (1985) *Social Policy and Labour Markets: The Employment Role of Social Provision*, paper presented at the International Political Science Association Conference in Paris, July.

Rich, A. (1980) *On Lies, Secrets and Silence*, Virago, London.

Roberts, G. (1978) 'The explanation of politics: comparison, strategy and theory' in P. G. Lewis *et al* (eds) *The Practice of Comparative Politics* 2nd ed, Longmans, London.

Rohrlich-Leavitt, R. (ed.) (1975) *Women Cross-Culturally: Change & Challenge*, Mouton Press, Hawthorne, NY.

Rose, R. (1984) *Do Parties Make A Difference?*, Macmillan, London (2nd ed).

Rowbotham, S. (1971) *Women, Resistance and Revolution*, Allen Lane, London.

Rowbotham, S. (1972) *Women's Consciousness, Man's World*, Penguin, Harmondsworth.

Rowbotham, S. (1979) *Beyond the Fragments*, Merlin Press, London.

Ruggie, M. (1983) *The State and Working Women*, Princeton University Press, New Jersey.

Rule, W. (1981) 'Why women don't run: the critical contextual factors in women's legislative recruitment', *Western Political Quarterly* 34(1), March, 60–77.

Runciman, W. G. (1966) *Relative Deprivation and Social Justice*, Routledge & Kegan Paul, London.

Rustow, D. A. (1967) *A World of Nations*, Brookings Institute, Washington, DC.

Saris, W. and Stronkhorst, H. (1984) *Causal Modelling in Nonexperimental Research*, Sociometric Research Foundation, Amsterdam.

Sawhill, I. (1976) 'Discrimination and poverty among women who head families' in M. Blaxall *et al* (eds) *Women and the Workplace*, Univ. of Chicago Press, Chicago.

Schfran, L. H. (1982) 'Women: reversing a decade of progress' in A. Gartner, C. Greer and F. Riessman (eds) *What Reagan is doing to Us*, Harper & Row, New York.

Schlegel, A. (ed.) (1977) *Sexual Stratification: A Crosscultural View*, Columbia University Press, New York.

Schmidt, M. (1985) *The Politics of Labour Market Policy*, paper delivered at the International Political Science Association, Paris.

Scott, H. (1984) *Working your Way to the Bottom: The Feminisation of Poverty*, Pandora Press, London.

Scott, H. (1982) *Sweden's Right to be Human*, Allison and Busby, London.

Semyonov, M. (1980) 'The social context of women's labor force participation: a comparative analysis', *American Journal of Sociology* 86(3), 534–50.

Seward, G. H. and Williamson, R. C. (1970) *Sex Roles in Changing Society*, Random House, New York.

Sharkansky, I. and Hofferbert, R. (1968) 'Dimensions of state politics, economics and public policy', *American Political Science Review* 63 (33), 867–80.

Sharkansky, I. (1968) *Policy Analysis in Political Science*, Markham, Chicago.

Sharpe, L. J. (1981) 'Does Politics Matter?' in K. Newton (ed.) *Urban Political Economy*, Pinter, London.

Sharpe, L. J. and Newton, K. (1984) *Does Politics Matter?* Cambridge, Cambridge University Press.

Simms, M. (1984) 'A women's place is in the House and in the Senate: women and the 1983 Australian elections', Political Studies Association Conference, Southampton.

Skaard, T. (1981) 'Progress for women: increased female representation in political élites in Norway' in Epstein, C. F. and Coser, R. L. (ed.) *Access to Power: Cross-National Studies of Women and Elites*, Allen & Unwin, London.

Smyth, A. (1984) 'Women and power in Ireland: problems, progress and practice', Second International Congress on Women, Groningen.

Spence, J. T. and Helreich, R. L. (1972) 'The attitudes towards women scale', *Journal of Applied Social Psychology* 2, 66.

Spender, D. (1981) *Men's Studies Modified*, Pergamon, Oxford.

Spender, D. (1985) *For the Record*, The Women's Press, London.

Stallard, K., Ehrenreich, B. and Sklar, H. (1983) *Poverty in the*

American Dream: Women and Children First, Institute for New Communications, South End Press, Boston.

Steiner, S. (1977) *The Female Factor*, Intercultural Press, USA.

Stevenson, M. (1978) 'Wage difference between men and women: economic theories' in Stromberg and Harkess *Women Working*, Mayfield, USA.

Sutherland, M. (1981) *Sex Bias in Education*, Blackwell, Oxford.

Szalai, A. (1975) 'The situation of women in the light of contemporary time-budget research', UN World Conference for International Women's Year, Mexico City.

Sweet, J. A. (1973) *Women in the Labour Force*, Seminar Press, New York.

Szalai, A. (1972) *The Use of Time*, Moulton, The Hague.

Szalai, A. (1975) *The Time Situation of Women in the Light of Contemporary Time Budget Research*, UN World Conference for International Women's Year, Mexico City.

Tietz, C. (1979) *Induced Abortion*, Population Council, New York.

Tiger, L. (1970) *Men in Groups*, Nelson, London.

Tinker, I, Bramson, M. B. and Buvinic, M. (eds) (1976) *Women and World Development*, Praeger, New York.

Treiman, D. J. (1977) *Occupational Prestige in Comparative Perspective*, Academic Press, USA.

UNESCO (Annual) *Statistical Yearbook*, UNESCO, Geneva.

United Nations (Annual) *Demographic Yearbooks*, United Nations, New York.

United Nations (1980a) *Report of the World Conference of the United Nations Decade for Women*, Copenhagen, A/CONF. 94–35.

United Nations (1980b) *The Economic Role of Women in the ECE Region*, United Nations, New York.

United Nations (1982a) *Economic Survey of Europe*, United Nations, New York.

United Nations (1982b) *World Population Trends and Policies*, United Nations, New York.

United Nations (1984a) *Compiling Social Indicators on the Situation of Women*, United Nations, New York.

United Nations (1984b) *Improving Concepts and Methods for Statistics and Indicators on the Situation of Women*, United Nations, New York.

United Nations (1984c) *Recent Levels and Trends of Contraceptive Use as Assessed in 1983*, United Nations, New York.

United Nations (1985a) *Review and Appraisal: World Conference to Review and Appraise the Achievements of the United Nations*

Decade for Women: Equality, Development and Peace, Nairobi, July, A/CONF. 116/5.

United Nations (1985b) *Selected Statistics and Indicators on the Status of Women* Report of the Secretary-General, World Conference to Review and Appraise the Achievements of the United Nations Decade for Women: Equality, Development and Peace, Nairobi A/CONF. 116/10.

United Nations (1985c) *Women's Rights*, United Nations, Vienna.

United States (1983) *Women at Work*, Department of Labour, Bureau of Labour Statistics, Bulletin 2168, Washington, D.C.

Vallance, E. and Davies, E. (1986) *Women of Europe: Women MEPs and Equality Policy*, Cambridge University Press, Cambridge.

Vallance, E. (1979) *Women in the House*, Athlone Press, London.

Van Dusen, R. A. and Sheldon, E. B. (1976) 'The changing status of American women: a life cycle perspective', *American Psychologist* 31, 106–16.

Verba, S. (1971) *Modes of Democratic Participation: A Cross National Comparison*, Sage, Beverly Hills.

Vogel-Polsky, E. (1985) *National Institutional and Non-Institutional Machinery established in the Council of Europe Member States to Promote Equality Between Women and Men*, Council of Europe, Strasbourg.

Walmsley, P. (1982) 'Women, feminism and the political process', *Politics* 17 (2), November, 65–9.

Warner, H. (1984) 'EC social policy in practice: community action on behalf of women and its impact in the member states', *Journal of Common Market Studies* XXIII(2) December, 141–67.

Welch, S. (1977) 'Women as political animals?', *American Journal of Political Science* 21(4), November.

Wilensky, H. L. (1975) *The Welfare State and Equality*, University of California Press, Calif.

Wilensky, H. L. (1968) 'Women's work, economic growth, ideology and structure', *Industrial Relations* 7(3) May.

World Bank (1983) *World Tables II*, Johns Hopkins Press, London.

World Bank (1983) *World Development Report*, Oxford University Press, Oxford.

Youssef, N. H. and Hartley, S. F. (1979) 'Demographic indicators on the status of women in various societies' in J. L. Blumen and J. Bernard *Sex Roles and Social Policy*, Sage, USA.

Index